~✖ FROM ✖~
CLOISTERS
to CUBICLES

Spiritual Disciplines for the Not-So-Monastic Life

DAVID SRYGLEY

WESTBOW®
PRESS
A DIVISION OF THOMAS NELSON
& ZONDERVAN

Scripture quotations taken from the New American Standard Bible®, Copyright © 1960, 1962, 1963, 1968, 1971, 1972, 1973, 1975, 1977, 1995 by The Lockman Foundation. Used by permission. (www.Lockman.org)

Epigraph: Geffrey B. Kelly and F. Burton Nelson, eds., *A Testament to Freedom: The Essential Writings of Dietrich Bonhoeffer* (San Francisco: Harper, 1990), 205.

WestBow Press books may be ordered through booksellers or by contacting:

WestBow Press
A Division of Thomas Nelson & Zondervan
1663 Liberty Drive
Bloomington, IN 47403
www.westbowpress.com
1 (866) 928-1240

ISBN: 978-1-4908-6724-3 (sc)
ISBN: 978-1-4908-6725-0 (hc)
ISBN: 978-1-4908-6723-6 (e)

Library of Congress Control Number: 2015901089

Printed in the United States of America.

WestBow Press rev. date: 2/3/2015

The restoration of the Church must surely depend on a new kind of monasticism, having nothing in common with the old but a life of uncompromising adherence to the Sermon on the Mount in imitation of Christ.

Dietrich Bonhoeffer

CONTENTS

Appendices

FOREWORD

Deep-rooted conceptions are difficult to change. But that is what David Srygley wants to help us achieve with this excellent book about spiritual disciplines. He believes the most common misunderstanding about spiritual disciplines is that they are about *detaching* from the world; he insists that they are about *engaging* the world.

To facilitate this change of conception in his readers, David analyzes twelve Spiritual Disciplines in a growth process he terms "reintegration," devoting a chapter to each of the twelve.

The first six are Preparatory, engendering individual growth: Prayer, Study, Meditation, Fasting, Simplicity, and Solitude and Silence. The remaining six are Engaging, zeroing in on the relational aspect of the Christian life to this world: Submission, Service, Confession, Worship, Guidance, and Celebration.

His foundational scriptures for these Spiritual Disciplines are two of the most difficult-to-achieve sentences in the Bible:

> ... *we are taking every thought captive to the obedience of Christ (2 Cor. 10:5).*

> ... *with humility of mind regard one another as more important than yourselves" (Phil. 1:3).*

The first is the recurring theme in all the disciplines. The second is the focus of the corporate or engaging disciplines.

David has carefully structured the order of the disciplines. Following that order is certainly the most effective path; in fact, he occasionally warns that a given discipline cannot be fully achieved without incorporating elements examined in previous ones. Even so, I came away feeling that this engaging book will meet you where you are. If you are a beginner it will give you a place to start. If you have already progressed from milk to meat it will provide a map for spiritual growth that can keep you absorbed for a lifetime. I find that each chapter works well as a stand-alone unit. So if one calls out to your particular need-of-the-moment, go straight to it; you can do the backfill work later.

David is a well-trained scholar and a remarkably gifted communicator. His passion for clarity is manifest in a writing style that is concise, crisp, and clear.

That isn't to say that you will always be comfortable. You won't be. (The chapters on Submission and Guidance had me nodding my head in agreement, but squirming.) You will experience "growing pains"—these are, after all, disciplines. But you will negotiate the terrain under the tutelage of a teacher with a gentle heart and nurturing spirit.

Each chapter ends with David offering a series of questions and journaling suggestions that help internalize and personalize the material—also providing an excellent guide for those who may choose to use the material in a class or group setting. For a compact view of the goals of this work I point you to David's own words at the end of the Preface.

I enthusiastically endorse both the material and the author. I hope you will use it and share it.

—Joe Barnett

PREFACE

Allow me, if I may, to begin at the end—of the book. While most prefaces give the reader a quick overview of the writer's rationale, which we'll come to shortly, and the order of the book, I need to "preface" my preface. If you are reading this book as a teacher or, if you are not a teacher but you decide one day to try to share with others, please read Appendix Two. It may be that Appendix Two is one of the most important "chapters" in this book.

I realize that it doesn't make much sense to put the most important chapter in an appendix, but I'm afraid that if it came first, most readers wouldn't make it to Chapter Two. The appendix is about educational philosophy and paradigms, particularly as they relate to teaching spiritual discipline, and as such aren't critical if you are reading this as a student. But if you decide to use this book in a class or small group, please take the time to read Appendix Two.

Now, on to the real Preface.

This book is a product of a challenge laid down by one of my seminary professors. He rightly stated that most Christians struggle with the practice of spiritual disciplines because they sound too mystical and monastic. One of the reasons for this "sound" is that spiritual disciplines were once the domain of monks and mystics. And while the practice of spiritual disciplines have slowly left the monasteries, hermitages, and nunneries, the goals of the practices have remained firmly entrenched among the cloisters of the great abbeys. What is needed, according Dr. Donald Whitney, is a new and better, thoroughly Christian understanding of spiritual disciplines and a curriculum that is built upon it. I believe that this book provides at least a first effort at that new and better understanding and provides a curriculum for practicing spiritual disciplines in the light of that new paradigm.

As will be obvious, the curriculum is built around the same twelve disciplines identified by Richard Foster. Foster's book, *Celebration of Discipline*, has become the standard primer for those interested in spiritual disciplines. If you have not read his book, I'd recommend you do so, perhaps even before starting this one!

A second author has contributed to both my own work and to that of many others in the field of spiritual disciplines, Dallas Willard. Whereas Foster provides the toolbox for spiritual disciplines, Willard provides the textbook. Foster readily and graciously acknowledges his debt to Willard. Willard's thoughts, captured originally in *Spirit of the Disciplines*, provided a spiritual, theological, and philosophical foundation for the practice of spiritual disciplines that was decades before its time. However, as the study of spirituality and spiritual disciplines has advanced over the last thirty years, we have finally caught up with Dallas Willard!

From Cloisters to Cubicles is my contribution to extending the work of both of these men, Willard at a theological level and Foster at a practical level. It will be clear that I don't fall in line with everything they write, but appreciate the foundation they have laid. So if you have ever read Willard or Foster and attempted to practice spiritual disciplines under their tutelage and have come up short in the experience, perhaps *From Cloisters to Cubicles* will provide a new understanding of the goals of spiritual disciplines and a fresh approach to their practice.

The first chapter of this book discusses in some detail the essence of the new paradigm for the practice of spiritual disciplines. Chapters Two to Thirteen then provide new foundations for and practices of each of the classic spiritual disciplines. Appendix One is a short report on some research I conducted on the relationship between the practice of spiritual disciplines and evangelistic efforts. Not surprisingly, those who were actively studying and practicing spiritual disciplines were more active in evangelism than those who were not. The surprise is the magnitude of the difference, but I won't ruin the surprise by telling you the numbers now.

Whether you are teaching this material or studying for your own edification, I want you to be aware of the goals and objectives of this book. As you read and study, consider how these lessons will assist you in achieving these objectives.

1. Help you understand the Scriptural foundation for each discipline.
2. Make the principle of the discipline easy to understand in only a few basic ideas.
3. Provide a "real world" point of contact with the curriculum. (In other words, the discipline can be practiced daily in the real world and not just in a cloister or closet.)
4. Help you practice the discipline in a "real life" setting.
5. Help you see and reflect on the impact of the discipline on your walk with God.

Ultimately, the educational goals[1] are that you will:

1. Be committed to a life of high spirituality (faith integration).
2. Develop an "inner life" that reflects the character of and faith in God.
3. Become competent in integrating the principles of the spiritual disciplines into real world decisions.
4. Avoid the difficulties associated with ungodly decisions.
5. Enjoy the peace and maturity of a fully integrated life.
6. See God's hand and recognize God's will in all situations.

If you'd like to gain a better understanding of these goals and their origins, don't forget to read Appendix Two! In the meantime, enjoy your journey with God as you stroll deeper into the Kingdom Life.

---

[1] Adapted from the educational goals of Proverbs 1–9 as identified in Daniel Estes, *Hear, My Son: Teaching and Learning in Proverbs 1–9* (Downers Grove, IL: InterVarsity, 1997.

ACKNOWLEDGEMENTS

As with any book, the number of encouragers, contributors, and editors is many. So let me start by thanking everyone who has, in any way, made this book into a reality.

To a few special people, however, I am deeply indebted. Dr. Stanley Helton has walked alongside me through the many hours and months of conceptualizing, writing, proofing, and polishing my thoughts. He is a great friend, a devoted spiritual mentor, and an extraordinary scholar.

Drs. Beougher and Trentham, two of the best professors at The Southern Baptist Theological Seminary, have earned my respect and admiration through their tireless commitment to developing leaders and evangelists in the Kingdom of God. Both have contributed to the philosophical and scriptural foundations of the theology of spirituality and evangelism that underlie this work.

Last but foremost, to my lovely, patient, and understanding wife, Dianna, who supports my love of God, of scholarship, and of sharing the Word, I owe the greatest thanks. She has allowed me to pursue this work that is both a dream and a calling from God. I know that God has blessed me beyond measure because of her.

I hope this book does justice to all of the people who have lovingly supported its writing. Above all, I pray it glorifies God, his church, and his Word.

David Srygley
October 8, 2014

WHAT IS A CLOISTER ANYWAYS?

Fair enough question! After all, unless you've walked the hallowed halls of some Ivy League school or sat pondering the universe in an ancient monastery or abbey, you probably haven't heard the word very often. And even though it rhymes with oyster, the two are very unrelated.

The meaning of the word has evolved over centuries, and I mean *centuries*, of use. The cloisters were, and still are, the long, open porches that serve as hallways around the garden located in the center of a complex of connected buildings. If you've visited an older college or perhaps an old cathedral, you've probably seen them. You walk through the front of a building and then out of the back door, but instead of finding open land, you find yourself in a garden surrounded by other buildings. Sometimes there is a fountain or a prayer garden designed and dedicated for peace and tranquility. It's usually a very beautiful place.

Around the garden runs a covered walkway with beautiful pillars supporting exquisitely hand-hewn archways. The walkway is open to the garden through any of the archways. In the days before air conditioning, this open design was a blessing to those who traveled through these buildings.

Great! So why name a book after a piece of architecture? Again, fair question!

Along the walls of the cloisters opposite the garden are doors to rooms of various size and uses. In their secular use, you might find offices, dining rooms, or bedrooms in no particular order. But as this design became used by more and more churches, abbeys, and monasteries, the rooms and their arrangement began to take on special meaning. In particular was the prayer room, usually found at the far end of the cloister. It was placed there to provide maximum solitude and silence to the religious practitioners who worshipped there.

This particular room, and its particular purpose of solitude, silence, prayer, and meditation, slowly began to commandeer the word cloister for its own use. A monk who was in need of prayer or isolation would go down the cloister pathway to the little room for prayer—which became known as the cloister room, or cloister. It was here, in the cloister, that monks and mystics and priests and others sought to strengthen their spiritual lives. Over time the cloister came to represent that place where a Christian would go to escape the world and strengthen his or her spiritual life and commitment.

Spiritual disciplines developed, or should I say resurfaced, during these times. The need to escape was partnered with a need to exercise godliness through the practice of many and varied disciplines, from fasting to outright starvation and from submissive service to self-flagellation. It wasn't pretty, but it was very personal, so a cloister was a great idea.

And so today, the idea remains. When I'm facing a struggle, I find my own cloister. I find a place of escape where I can repair my spiritual life (or worse, lick my wounds) and then go back into the world. This works well because my spiritual life is a personal thing between me and God. It's best practiced in a closet, or cloister, or wherever no one else can see me. Once I get my spiritual life in order, I can return to the world and continue doing what I've always done, which usually amounts to nothing spiritual!

If you found yourself agreeing with the last paragraph (or most of it anyways), you suffer from cloisterism! I know, it's not a real word, but it sure sounds horrible! The symptoms of cloisterism are three-fold: (1) you've made your spirituality so personal and private that no one can see it, (2) you've failed to develop a spirituality that is viable in this world and, therefore, have to escape the world to practice it. (This goes for people who only think worship occurs in a church building on Sundays.), and (3) you think that this is the way God intended your spiritual life to be.

If this describes you, I hope this book can provide a cure for your "cloisterism." I hope you'll discover that your spiritual life was never meant to be lived "under a bushel" (Matt 5:15). I hope you'll discover a spiritual life that is filled with "power, love, and discipline" (2 Tim 1:7). And most of all, I hope you will reject the lukewarm, ineffective, unrewarding life that so many have accepted as "the Christian life" and chose instead to live the Kingdom Life Now!

This is where the cubicle comes in! This book is designed to move you from practicing your Christianity in a closet to living it out daily in every venue of life, including work, school, family, and even in the car! As you study these lessons, your Christian life should begin to take captive every arena of your life for "the obedience of Christ." Can you live as a Christian in your work environment? Sure you can, and this book will help you do it by moving your spiritual life *From Cloisters to Cubicles.*

THE ORIGINS OF THE UNIVERSE— OR AT LEAST SPIRITUAL DISCIPLINES

How would you define spirituality? It's an honest question that many of us have struggled with. While some may think the answer is rather ethereal (that's Greek for totally meaningless), I hope you'll find that it's neither meaningless nor unimportant.

For one thing, how we define spirituality directly impacts the way we understand spiritual disciplines. If we have an incorrect understanding of spirituality, we'll have an equally incorrect understanding of the purposes of spiritual disciplines—and even what spiritual disciplines are.

Many Christians have attempted to practice spiritual disciplines; most have struggled. Because the practice of spiritual disciplines originated in mysticism and monasticism, many traditional, mainstream Christians shy away from them. Those who have tried to practice them have met with mixed results. Most aren't even sure what they're trying to accomplish, so how could they possibly know if they did it right or well?

The goal of this first chapter, which happens to be one of the longest in the book, is to help you understand spirituality and spiritual disciplines in a biblical way. With a thoroughly scriptural foundation at our feet, the practice of spiritual disciplines can help every one of us achieve the walk with God that both he and we desire!

The Chicken and Egg Discussion

Before addressing spiritual disciplines, one must address the meaning of the word spirituality. This meaning is rather slippery. Many books have been written about many topics under the subject heading of spirituality. The definitions range considerably, but most people use it to refer to either the inner or otherworldly spiritual dimension of a person's life. In other words, we all have a spiritual dimension or realm to which we are in some way attached. Spirituality describes that realm or, perhaps, our lives when we are abiding in that realm. Though I don't think it was his intent, C. S. Lewis provided a glimpse into what this mindset might look like in his book, *The Great Divorce*.[2]

The problem with this view is that it's rooted in Dualism. Dualism is a philosophical system that teaches that the body and the spirit are, at best, incompatible, and at worst, antagonistic. While some Scripture can be cited in support of this view, it can certainly only be applied to our pre-Christian state (Rom 7:14-25). In our restored, born again life, any animosity between flesh and spirit has been crucified in the body of Christ on the cross (Eph 2:11-18). As a foundation for spirituality, this dualistic premise makes spirituality something to which you escape, further driving a wedge between one's day-to-day life and spiritual life.

Both mysticism and monasticism grew out of the perceived need to separate oneself from the physical world in order to attain to the spiritual world. Mystics pursued a more supernatural course of action while monastics (usually associated with monks and monasteries) chose a more pragmatic route. In either approach, practitioners were seeking to divorce themselves from the world around them to reach a higher, or fuller, spiritual life. And it's this view that has continued to shape and define the practice of spiritual disciplines. Even

---

[2] C. S. Lewis, *The Great Divorce* (New York: HarperCollins, 2001).

those who don't buy into mysticism or move into monasteries have accepted, usually unknowingly, practices of spiritual disciplines built upon Dualistic goals and philosophy.

Dualism in Action

Most people, when they think of disciplines, envision monks in closets or priests in drab brown robes flailing themselves with whips. For those who aren't so dramatic, the experience still seems, in our mind's eye, rather detached. After all, how does one meditate while driving to and from work ninety minutes each day, or fast when a family of four is waiting to be fed dinner, or celebrate when bills have to be paid and debt collectors have to be avoided? For most of us, practicing spiritual disciplines sounds like pie in the sky.

This monastic model, which implies separating ourselves from the world, didn't work well for the common Christian who had to feed their families and such. So the model was taken out of the monastery and brought into the real world. If people couldn't leave the world and go to a monastery, they were encouraged to at least try to get as much of the world out of their lives as possible. A simple illustration may help. For the majority of people, then and now, who lean towards the more mystical view, the goal of spiritual disciplines looked something like this:

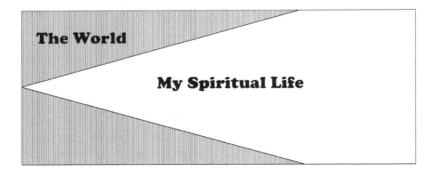

In this context, spiritual disciplines are the process by which the world is pushed out of our lives so that we can live free of its influence. Of course, the most direct way of achieving this was to simply move to a monastery!

Disciplines for the Common Man

What about those who don't want to live in monasteries and practice chants and enchantments? What reason could there be for them to consider such arduous practices as fasting, solitude, and sacrifice? For the Roman Catholic Church, the answer is clear; you need it for grace!

The Roman Catholic Church taught that salvation was something that had to be earned through means of grace. This term, "means of grace," has its origins in the Roman Catholic view that the grace received at conversion was only sufficient for immediate salvation from past sins (what we might call justification). In order to ensure eternal salvation (or sanctification), a Christian needed to earn grace. This was accomplished primarily through sacraments, but other "means of [obtaining] grace" were also available, such as charity, special sacrifices, and even indulgences.[3] Spiritual disciplines, over the course of time, also became a means by which Christians could merit additional grace. Needless to say, the Reformation view that Christ's grace is sufficient for all times didn't work well with this teaching.

Regardless of the Protestant dislike for "meriting grace," many mainstream Christian writers have largely maintained

---

[3] J. Waterworth, ed. and trans., "The Council of Trent: The Cannons and Decrees of the Sacred and Oecumenical Council of Trent (London: Dolman, 1848), 48-49, http://history.hanover.edu/texts/trent/ trentall. html (accessed October 21, 2013).

the language of "means of grace" and only slightly modified its meaning. Many Christians believe they can't earn saving grace, but they believe they can benefit from receiving more grace from God. Many writers on spiritual disciplines see those disciplines as means of attaining this extra measure of grace and the benefits thereof.

Donald S. Whitney uses a similar model, stating that spiritual disciplines are like "channels of transforming grace."[4] In his view, our lives are meant to be filled with the power of God. When the various aspects of our lives, such as work, marriage, family, and church, are out of alignment with God's flow of grace, we don't receive the spiritual life intended for us.

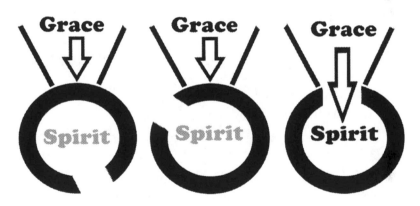

Our Spirit, and therefore our Spiritual Life, is disconnected from the Grace of God. The Grace we need for empowering our Spirit and our Spiritual Life cannot flow into our lives and Spirit until we align our lives with the will of God.

Spiritual disciplines, then, aid Christians by helping them bring their lives into alignment with God's will. The result is that we can be filled with a measure of spiritual strength beyond our understanding and control.

---

[4] Donald Whitney, *Spiritual Disciplines for the Christian Life* (Colorado Springs: NavPress, 1991), 17.

This model is a step in the right direction. Instead of viewing spiritual disciplines as means of escaping this world or separating ourselves from life, this model views spiritual disciplines as means of connecting our physical world with the spiritual world in order to receive the transforming power of God. Unfortunately, even in this model, the Dualistic undertones remain. The spiritual world becomes more accessible, but remains separate.

How Could Spiritual Disciplines Serve Christians Better?

So what if we changed our vision for spiritual disciplines? What if spiritual disciplines aren't about getting anything? Would spiritual disciplines take on new meaning and new appeal if we understood them in a more practical sense? I believe they would. Instead of closet-bound, early-morning, mystical experiences, spiritual disciplines can become all-day, every-day faith exercises by which Christ's likeness becomes a greater reality in our lives.

Dallas Willard, departing from the ancient models and even the derived Protestant model, proposed views of spirituality and spiritual disciplines that are much more Scriptural. At the core of Willard's view is the understanding that the spiritual realm and the worldly realm have been torn apart. Two realms never meant to be separated have been! I call this phenomenon dis-integration.

While disintegration likely brings to mind images of Martian death rays, that isn't exactly what I mean. Disintegration is the breaking down of a whole (integer) into little bitty pieces. (Okay, so the atomization of the Martian death ray actually isn't too far off!) For us as humans, sin has disintegrated us because the very fiber of our existence was our *imago Dei*, or image of God, in which we were made and which is now corrupted by sin. What once was a complete being (more on this in a minute) is now, in Willard's terminology, a disembodied self. The physical self is separated from the spiritual self, but contrary to Dualism, this is an unnatural state that needs to be corrected. In other words, the spiritual and physical lives need to be reintegrated into a single life.

A Few New Definitions

Building on Willard's work, we can begin to redefine every aspect of the discussion on spiritual disciplines, beginning with a new definition of spirituality. If the spiritual life is not supposed to be separate from the physical life, it becomes impossible to discuss spirituality in any sense that does not include the physical life as an integral part. In other words, any concept of spirituality must be fully spiritual and fully physical. This truth should come as no surprise since spirituality is generally associated with transformation into the likeness of Christ, who, in his incarnation, was 100 percent God and 100 percent Man.

The definition that meets this criterion is a rather simple one. Spirituality is the integration of one's faith and one's whole life. To put it in measurable terms, individuals would possess a high degree of spirituality if they interpret and respond to everything in their life according to what they believe about God (Heb 5:11-14). The opposite is intuitively true; those who choose to make decisions based on anything other than their faith we consider unspiritual.

By reenvisioning spirituality as something that engages and captures the world, this illustration becomes better:

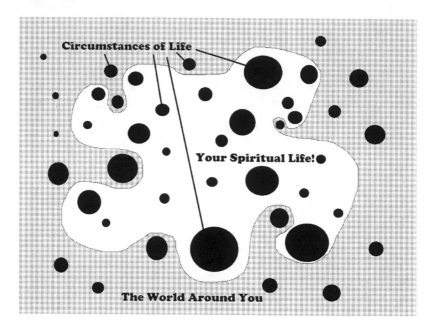

While not as smooth and clean as a well-oiled machine (life never is, right?), this revised view is supported by two important verses, "and we are taking every thought captive to the obedience of Christ" (2 Cor 10:5) and "but he who is spiritual appraises all things" (1 Cor 2:15). In this view, Christians must remain in the world. However, unlike the mystical, monastic model, Christians learn to "take every thought captive." We take each thought and situation captive by appraising everything through the lens of our newly recreated, spiritual beings. Spiritual disciplines, in this view, are the exercises in our Christian life that help bring every aspect of our life under the reign of Christ in our lives (a.k.a. "the obedience of Christ"). In other words, they facilitate integration and transformation!

This integration, however, isn't simply a matter of willing ourselves to make the right choices; it requires a transformation of our very selves into something remarkably

Christ-like. Paul, in Romans 7:14-25, states that knowing and desiring isn't enough; something has to change on the inside. That change, or transformation, is our salvation in Christ (Rom 7:25—8:2). Yet even after our conversion, there is an expectation of continuing growth and transformation through the renewing of our minds (Rom 12:1-2). The results of the renewing, or making our mind and life like it was before it was disintegrated, is that we are no longer conformed to this world or the patterns of thoughts that control it—and us!

The goal of that growth and transformation is godliness. Because we understand, at least intuitively, that increasing levels of spirituality parallel increased godliness, the term "godliness" is often used as a synonym for spirituality. We think, "If someone is very spiritual then she is very godly." Almost immediately our experiences tell us that this isn't always true, even though our minds tell us it should be. Why then is there a discrepancy? I believe it's because we have been working with the wrong definition of spirituality.

The old definition allows for someone to possess a distinctive otherworldliness that we perceive as spiritual, but whose life is not distinctively Christian. However, if we consider our definition of spirituality as a level of integration of faith and life, then godliness becomes the observable outcome of that integration. In other words, those who have a high degree of spirituality are those who make decisions based on faith, which in turn, manifests godliness in their daily lives. When Paul discusses the fruit of the Spirit (Gal 5:22-23), perhaps he is referring to the results of allowing the Spirit to direct how we live and make decisions.

As we consider the transformation that is expected, the integration that is necessary, and the godliness that is the result, we find we have stumbled upon a good biblical definition of maturity as well. When we speak of spiritual maturity we are talking about the level of competency a

9

Christian has in integrating faith with the real world. If this sounds like maturity and spirituality are the same thing, that's because they almost are! Remember, spirituality is not exactly a biblical term, even though a principle of spirituality is certainly implied in Scripture. What is a biblical term is *teleos*, which is translated maturity, completeness, or perfection. The Bible tells us exactly what mature Christians are. They are those who "have trained their senses to discern good and evil" (Heb 5:14). Through experience, discipline, and knowledge of God's Word, mature Christians have learned to integrate fully and completely their faith into every decision that they make, thereby allowing them to discern good and evil.

The Role of Spiritual Disciplines

This recognition of our need for on-going transformation through the reintegration of faith and life brings us to spiritual disciplines. Spiritual disciplines are practices or exercises in the life of a Christian that aid him or her in the transformation process. Spiritual disciplines should help Christians integrate faith into their daily lives. And while this process begins by bringing the spiritual world back into our physical lives, ultimately the goal is to tip the scale. As reintegration occurs, we should reach a point when we are no longer living as physical beings incorporating faith and spirituality, but spiritual being taking the world captive by our faith.

If we consider the fact that most practitioners of spiritual disciplines have historically been mystics, monks, and hermits, one might think detaching oneself from the world is the goal. When we consider the nature of prayer, fasting, meditation, solitude, and simplicity, how could disciplines be about anything other than detaching from the world? This is perhaps the most common misunderstanding of spiritual disciplines.

If we look at the examples of Christ and the disciples, when we do see them practicing some of the spiritual disciplines, it's to prepare themselves to engage the world. Jesus fasted before beginning his ministry (Matt 4). He prayed before he went to the cross (Luke 22). The church at Antioch, including Barnabas and Saul, prayed and fasted before appointing Barnabas and Saul to their first missionary journey (Acts 13:2-3). Spiritual disciplines are not for escaping the world; *they are for engaging it!*

This spirit of engagement lies at the heart of Willard's conceptualization of spirituality and spiritual disciplines. Most of us are familiar with Foster's threefold division of spiritual disciplines: inward, outward, and corporate.[5] Willard groups his discussion of spiritual disciplines into only two categories, disciplines of abstinence, which include such things as silence and solitude, fasting, and meditation, and disciplines of engagement, such as service, celebration, and worship.[6] Unfortunately, the idea of engagement has been overlooked or misapplied by many people seeking to practice spiritual disciplines. And even though ministries such as Renovaré are moving engagement to the forefront of spirituality, we still need to better define what engagement means for Christians.

I believe part of reformulating the idea of spiritual disciplines involves identifying a better twofold division. While I don't disagree with the practices Willard placed in disciplines of abstinence, I think disciplines of preparation would be a much

---

[5] Richard Foster, *Celebration of Discipline: The Path to Spiritual Growth*, 3rd ed. (San Francisco: Harper, 1998).

[6] Dallas Willard, *The Spirit of the Disciplines* (San Francisco: Harper & Row, 1988), 158.

better name. In this way, we realize some of the more arduous, contemplative tasks prepare us for the next step in, and ultimate purpose of, spiritual disciplines—engaging the world!

Spiritual Transformation

If spiritual disciplines are, as I believe, the exercises by which faith and life are reintegrated to produce our wholeness with and in God, they cannot be optional. Spiritual discipline is the heart of spiritual transformation, and spiritual disciplines are the cardiovascular exercises that make transformation possible and our spiritual lives healthy ones. Because of a lack of spiritual exercise, Christians are dying daily from "heart" disease—unhealthy, atrophied spiritual lives.

The Apostle Peter, in his second letter, helps bring together the idea of spiritual growth, godliness, and reintegration. After our initial faith, Peter declares grace and peace "be multiplied" or "abound" to us in the true knowledge of Christ. The more we know, the more we grow in the blessings of God. He further reminds us that true knowledge results in godliness, and that "these things" work together to make us "partakers of the divine nature." As we grow in knowledge, receive the blessings of God, and develop a life of godliness, we gain the power to escape the corruption of this world and reclaim our spiritual integrity through participation in the divine nature!

This model revolves around a simple truth. Spiritual disciplines must be practical. They must help us live godly lives. They must help us escape the corruption that is in this world, though not the world itself. ("In" and not "Of," right?) They must help us reintegrate the divine nature, lost through sin, with our lives today. They must empower us to engage the world, not escape the world!

Process of Reintegrative Spiritual Transformation
(2 Peter 1:1-4)

Conversion (Faith) →

Growth and Fullness through Spiritual Disciplines
(Grace and Peace Multiplied in True Knowledge) →

Godliness (Life and Godliness) →

Mature Spirituality
(Escaped the Corruption that is in this World by Lust) →

Spiritually Reintegrated Beings
(Become Partakers of Divine Nature)

Personal Practices

Now, let's try this again!

1. How would you define "spirituality"? How has that definition changed as a result of this first lesson?

2. What do you think of when you hear "spiritual disciplines"? How has that changed?

3. What do you think is the purpose of spiritual disciplines? What benefits does a person derive from them? How has your view of spiritual disciplines change?

Journal Reflections

If you keep a journal, and I hope you either do or will start, spend the week reflecting on three key passages of the model presented in this lesson. How does each contribute to an understanding of spirituality and spiritual disciplines as methods of engaging the world?

2 Corinthians 10:5

1 Corinthians 2:15

2 Peter 1:1-4

PRAYER

Preparation for Life—With All Its Challenges

My daughter participated in high jump in high school. She was okay at it, but she also demonstrated the potential to be better. One of the coaches at church offered to give her a few lessons. The two or three lessons were invaluable, but the first was the most important—how to jump! For all of us who have skipped rope, bounced on trampolines, or jumped over our small children who always seem to be underfoot, jumping would seem to be easy. As it turns out, jumping is a science. There is a logical progression to a full-body jump: hand, head, torso, hips, and then legs. If you don't jump with and through all of the body parts, you won't have a good jump.

Spiritual growth is a product of spiritual exercise. Especially in the beginning, that exercise should be accomplished in a particular order if it's to be effective. That's not to say that you may not need more of one type of exercise than another, something we'll discuss later, but you should try to progress in a reasonable way. For spiritual growth to occur, that order begins with prayer.

If you have read Richard Foster's book, *Celebration of Discipline*, you know that he begins with the discipline of meditation. While this may work for some people, I believe every endeavor we undertake as Christians should begin with prayer. Meditation and fasting better serve as supplements to a good prayer life, and not the other way around.

We've all been to the mall during Christmas. The only line longer than the toy store is the line to get your picture made with Santa. But truthfully, the kids don't care about the picture. They want to make sure that Santa knows what they want for Christmas. Imagine, if you can do this, a child who crawls up on Santa's lap, gives him a great, big toothy smile (minus the proverbial two front teeth), and cuddles up next to the warm, red suit. Then Santa asks the obligatory, "What would you like for Christmas, little girl?" The girl replies, and this is when your imagination really has to go into overdrive, "Nothing. All I want for Christmas is you." Okay, I know I'm verging on copyright infringement, so I have to be careful, but you get the point. Her greatest wish was just to cuddle up with Santa. What if that were true when we came before God in prayer?

The apostle Paul assures us that if we are in need of God's strength, the Holy Spirit will help us come into his presence. In Romans 8:26-27 we are reminded that the Spirit helps us in our time of weakness. The Holy Spirit doesn't need a list from us. In fact, he works best when he "intercedes for us with groaning too deep for words" (Rom 8:26). Perhaps Paul understood that the greatest value in prayer was being ushered into the presence of God on the wings of the Holy Spirit, and not getting to be next in line to make our requests of the Father.

The differences between sitting with Santa and coming before the Lord in prayer are what happen afterwards. First, Santa gets tucked away for 330 days. I hope that is not true of your time with God! Second, after a cuddly visit with Santa, we leave with the warm fuzzies. After time spent in the presence of God, we leave with new strength and boldness.

Consider the prayer of Peter and his companions in Acts 4:23-31. Peter and John had been released from prison and told never to speak of Jesus again. Their reply was simple, "Yeah, right! Do you really think we're going to listen to you instead of God?" And so they returned to share with their friends what had happened.

The prayer that was lifted up by everyone is wonderful. Paraphrased, they said "God, we know that people are always going to fight against your truth and against your will—even though they can't do anything about it. Lord, use us mightily in your plan so that all the world may know" So God did! Verse 31 says, "And when they had prayed ... they were all filled with the Holy Spirit, and began to speak the word of God with boldness." When we come before God without a personal agenda and ask him for the strength and boldness to do his will *regardless* of our needs, he will fill our lives with a spirit of "power and love and discipline" (2 Tim 1:7).

The other beauty of prayer is that it creates confidence in God. Peter and the others prayed for confidence to speak "while Thou doest extend Thy hand to heal, and signs and wonders take place through the name of Thy holy servant Jesus" (Acts 4:30). Prayer places us squarely in God's will, which means we can count on him to have our backs. When we go out into the world knowing that we are doing what God wants, we enjoy the confidence of knowing that he will do his part.

The Practice of Prayer

Prayer is to be learned. We all do prayer right the first time. Our salvation hinges on being able to humbly come before God and throw ourselves on his mercy. For some reason, it seems to go downhill from there. But we are not alone in this quandary. The disciples had to ask Jesus, "Teach us to pray" (Luke 11:1), even after having left everything to follow him.

Learning to pray is not about techniques; it's about placement. We must recognize God's holiness, God's provision, and our sinfulness. These three ideas capture the essence of the Lord's Prayer that is Jesus' answer to their request. Many long prayers have waxed eloquent about God's holiness, praised him for his gracious provision, and bemoaned man's woeful state of sin. Unfortunately, the pray-er, while believing everything he said, had not learned to place his life before God as an unrighteous sinner before a holy God on whom he must rely. Prayer isn't about getting words in the right order; it's about getting a life in the right order.

Foster writes, "Openness, honesty, and trust mark the communication of children with their father."[7] As we learn to be open, honest, and trusting of our heavenly Father, our prayers will improve and our lives will grow. But these three "marks" aren't easy. They imply, among other things, that Christians must open themselves completely to God. For prayer to be effective, we must allow God access to every nook and cranny of our lives. But this makes perfectly good sense. God cannot refresh and restore what is not offered to him to do so! So again, learning to pray isn't about a technique; it's learning to let God in your life.

Prayer is to be imaginative. This isn't a biblical concept *per se.* The Bible doesn't say, "Thou shalt use thy imagination when ye cometh before the Lord in solemn prayer." However, Old Testament Wisdom Literature is full of images, creativity, analogies, stories, etc. These techniques powerfully conveyed God's sovereignty, majesty, and loving-kindness. So why wouldn't they work for us today?

---

[7] Foster, *Celebration*, 40.

Think about our Santa story. You didn't have any trouble envisioning the little girl in Santa's lap. What if the same story were told again, but instead of Santa's lap it was Jesus' lap? Would you feel just as cozy? Would you still want to cuddle up next to your Savior and Shepherd?

Prayer is to be fine-tuned. Some people are better at "public" prayers than others. Some have a stronger personal prayer life than others. People are just at different points in their walk with God, and it shows in their prayers. They have learned, through practice and experience, to adjust their prayers in two ways.

First, they have prayed enough to know what works for them. Their image of Jesus and his compassion are very real for them. This may not have been the case when they began their prayer life. They may have had the same brown, gold, and white picture of Jesus holding a lamb that you do right now. But over time, they've adjusted it to be more personal—and refreshing.

Second, they learned to adjust their prayers to the situation in which it's needed. There was once a young man who visited a church on Sunday morning. At the end of the service, an older man got up and "worded" a wonderful prayer. The young man was awe-struck at the man's eloquence and even mentioned so to the local preacher. The preacher replied, "Yes indeed, that prayer was very good, but you ought to hear his other one." Having two prayers is NOT what I mean. As we learn to pray, we learn how to bring anything and everything before God.

We often wonder about the prayer of Jesus in the Garden of Gethsemane (Luke 22:42). Was he showing us his "human" side? Was he trying to back out of God's plan? Was it just for show so that we'd know how to pray? I think it was an honest prayer that was absolutely appropriate for his situation in life. It didn't have all the flourish of the model prayer he had taught his disciples, but it matched the situation perfectly. "Father," he said, "I know this isn't going to be easy. If there is another way, let's try it. If not, we'll do it your way and not mine. Amen." Try to think of another prayer that would have been more appropriate than that one. I can't do it.

Prayer is also fine-tuned by the Holy Spirit. Remember the Spirit's promise to "intercede for us with groaning too deep for words" (Rom 8:26)? Times will come when no model, no thought, no imagination, no experience will produce the right words in our hearts. It's then that we can trust the promise of God to be there and pray with us.

Prayer is to be continual. Paul says to pray without ceasing. Jesus says to ask for *daily* bread. New Testament Christians are to be in prayer always. Does that mean we should always be "asking for stuff" or always be "seeking refreshment from God"? If prayer is a time of refreshing, then we can be praying simply by dwelling in his warm, cozy presence. If we remain in the presence of God, when we do need to ask him for something, he's right there for us!

Daily Living

Prayer as a spiritual discipline becomes foundational to our growth. Jesus tells us that he is the vine and we are the branches, "he who abides in Me, and I in him, he bears much fruit; for apart from Me you can do nothing" (John 15:5). Prayer *is* the spirit of abiding in him. It's the foundation of all spiritual fruit, including our own spiritual growth.

So how can abiding prayer help us to "take every thought captive for obedience to Christ"? Think of prayer as a spider's web. As we abide in prayer in the presence of God, we weave a web of spiritual thoughts. Our thoughts become focused on the thoughts of God—which is why the Bible is such a help in this process, but more on that later! Soon, the thoughts of God become our thoughts. (I believe this is exactly what Paul means by the "renewing of our minds" in Romans 12:2.) Now, when we encounter new thoughts and situations and circumstances, they are captured, processed, and assimilated into our lives through the dual lenses of Scripture and Spirit.

For example, you are sitting at your desk working on an expense report for your last business trip. Maybe as you begin, you think to thank God for your job which he has provided. As you work through the receipts, you run across the bill from the restaurant where you took your client. You remember a few off-colored jokes you told to "lighten the mood." You ask for forgiveness and make a note to apologize to the client later. As you wrap up the report to give to your boss, you remember that she's been really struggling with her pregnancy, so you lift her up in prayer. As you turn in the report to her, you ask her how she's doing. You spend a few minutes visiting with her and encouraging her. You even let her know you'll be praying for her and her baby. You leave her office. In the course of maybe two hours, you've used an expense report, a receipt, and a short visit to glorify and thank God. That's abiding prayer taking every thought captive in its spiritual web!

Personal Practices

1. Begin approaching God in your prayers for refreshment or renewal, not for "getting."

2. Use your "nearness" and "refreshing" to decipher daily situations instead of waiting until your "prayer time" before bed (or whenever you return to your cloister!)

Journal Reflections

1. Imagine God, or Jesus. Imagine what it would be like to physically approach him. How are you feeling? Now imagine a warm smile and an inviting gesture. Picture yourself crawling up into Jesus' lap, cuddling next to him, and just resting there. How are you feeling now? Develop this image thoroughly in your mind and in your journal. Keep that image with you throughout the week. As you encounter life, imagine looking up into the eyes of Jesus. What and how would you ask him at that moment?

2. Consider obstacles to approaching God and to accepting his direction in your life. Write down a few of those obstacles each day. How might drawing near to God help you gain confidence in overcoming those obstacles? Try some ways of drawing near in prayer and write down the outcomes.

STUDY

Allowing God to Transform
Our Lives by Transforming Our Vision

I f you have kids, you've experienced this phenomenon. You give your child crystal clear instructions on how to clean his room. You leave; you return, and nothing is done correctly. Surprised (though honestly I don't know why!), you ask the famous—and usually rhetorical—question, "Did I not make myself perfectly clear?" Your child answers with the same blank stare that often accompanies a child caught in some unfortunate situation; what we call the "deer-in-the-headlights look" down South. He appears to have no idea what you are talking about!

The truth is that he has no idea what you are talking about. In some cases you can attribute this lack of attention to detail to some form of attention-deficit disorder. In most cases, however, the problem is much simpler; he didn't listen to a word you said. Is it because you (and I, apparently) have rebellious, disrespectful, hard-headed, stiff-necked, dunces for children? Of course we don't. We have children for children. Your child didn't listen to your instructions for the same reason we don't listen to God's; we have already decided how we are going to clean our rooms.

The Word of God intersects every aspect of our lives. Unfortunately, many people do not believe this because they have so much trouble "finding verses that apply" to a specific situation. This statement represents two fallacies. First, most people *can* find a verse that applies to their situation; they just don't like what it says! This situation is much like the "cleaning the room" problem.

Secondly, the Bible doesn't apply to situations; it applies to Christians! The Bible isn't a solution manual like you may have had in a high school or college Algebra class; it's the textbook. And what happens to most students who use the solution manual instead of the textbook to answer the practice questions? They fail the tests. If we keep going to the Bible to get one answer at a time to one specific question of life, we fail to learn the principles of godliness that help us overcome temptation, stand strong under persecution, and find peace during hardships.

God's Word is Sufficient

One of the reasons that we treat the Bible like a solution manual is that we think it only relates to the "spiritual" problems of our life. If I want a stronger faith, I go to the Bible. If I want a better prayer life, I go to the Bible. If I want to be more successful in sales work, I go to Dale Carnegie. If I want to manage my money better, I go to Dave Ramsey. If I want to be a better parent, I go to James Dobson. In a disconcerting sense, we have become like the Israelites of the Old Testament; we have a "god" for each need of our life. Instead of Baal, Asheroth, Yahweh, and Dagon, we have Zig Ziglar, Dr. Joyce Brothers, Peter Drucker, and God.

The challenge set before us as Christians is to rely completely and only on God's Word. How can we do so if there appears to be so many situations that the Bible doesn't address? This attitude begs the bigger question. Should we be in those situations in the first place? In Isaiah 55:11 God states very clearly, "So shall My word be which goes forth from My mouth; It shall not return to Me empty, Without accomplishing what I desire, And without succeeding *in the matter* for which I sent it." God's words *always* works! But there is a subtle qualifier hidden within this verse. God's word always works to accomplish what God desires.

This fact has two implications. First, this verse means that God's words cannot be used to accomplish what we desire—unless we desire what God desires. Christians who "consult" the Bible to determine how to get what they want will come up short every time. The Bible cannot successfully direct your life unless your life is squarely in the will of God.

This truth leads to the second implication. When we find ourselves in situations that the Bible doesn't address, it may be that we are in situations we were never meant to be in! Obviously these two ideas are closely tied. If I am doing everything my way, then the mess I discover I am in isn't God's fault. Nor then should we blame the Bible for not having the immediate solution. To carry out our solution manual analogy, you're trying to use an algebra solution manual in an organic chemistry class! You have double trouble. You are in a situation you shouldn't be trying to use the Bible in a way it can't be!

I want to make clear that being in a difficult situation does not always mean that you are not in God's will. Job is a good example of a man in God's will whose situation seemed pretty hopeless. However, when we are in a situation that we know we created through disobedience, the Bible isn't going to say, "Go up here and take a left. Travel forty feet and turn right. Apologize to the first person you see." The Bible *is* going to say, "Repent and follow God."

When Paul writes his second letter to Timothy (3:16-17), the apostle states, "All Scripture is inspired by God and profitable for teaching, for reproof, for correction, for training in righteousness; that the man of God may be adequate, equipped for every good work." Did you see that? The Bible equips us "for every *good* work." Does it equip us for "bad" work? Of course it doesn't. Bad work is not the purpose of God! But if you want to do "good" work, then learn from the Bible everything you can!

What if you are stuck in the middle of some really bad works? Can the Bible help you? Sure it can, but not the way most people want it to. Most people want to "get out of trouble" but aren't interested in doing or being good. So they look for a way to escape trouble without having to commit to living a 100% Christian life. They will be sorely disappointed for no such instructions exist. If you want to escape the snares of this world, you have to use the Bible to learn to live life God's way. Stated another way, the Bible won't teach you how to be lukewarm (Rev 3:16).

The Word of God is Light

John tells us that the Word came to earth and that, "In Him was life, and the life was the light of men. And the light shines in the darkness and darkness did not comprehend it" (John 1:4-5). We know that the Word to which he refers is Jesus (1:14), but that doesn't diminish the Word as the Bible. Just as Jesus is and speaks the Words of Life, the Bible is the record of those same words. And just as Jesus brought light into the darkness, the Word of God brings light to our paths (Psalms 119:105).

Like any light, though, the Word of God can be made ineffective. A lamp placed under a bushel provides no light

(Matt 5:15). A Bible tucked away on a shelf has the same result. Further, a flashlight is only useful when you shine it on the right something. A flashlight pointed at your face may make a scary shadow, but it won't help you safely through a dark corridor or help you find a lost coin in a dark room. Light works best when it's allowed to illuminate a space or an object.

So it is with the Word of God. Christians must learn to wield the light of God's Word with the same precision they wield the Word as the sword of the Spirit. But in this case, the light is for our own benefit. We must learn to shine it into the dark recesses of our soul. We must leave no thought free from the light of Christ. Every thought must be captured by the light and evaluated honestly and sincerely.

Yet men can read the Bible and still not "see" and experience the truth. How does that happen? For the Word of God to be effective, as Isaiah proclaims, it must be allowed to transform us "by the renewing of [our] mind" (Rom 12:2). The light of the Word of God must be shone, and applied, into every nook and cranny of our hearts and minds. We must begin to think and see differently. Remember, one of the premises of our study of spiritual disciplines is that they are to help us appraise all things as spiritual men and women (1 Cor 2:15). Our renewed minds, transformed by the Word of God, help us see and appraise *everything* in the light of God's Word.

More Than Study

I know a lot of very "Bible-smart" people. They can quote Scripture, wax eloquent on the Colossian Heresy, and defend Paul's authorship of Hebrews to the shame of many professors and preachers. What they can't do, or won't do, is take a few hours and shine all that knowledge on their own life circumstances. They know the Bible, but its message always remains at arm's length.

Richard Foster writes about a four-step understanding of Bible study that helps Christians use the Bible to shine God's light into our darkness.[8] The first step is *repetition*. While we grimace at the idea of repetition, with thoughts of endless Bible drills, books and verses to be memorized, and boring teachers repeating themselves unendingly, repetition serves a very important purpose. Foster calls it "ingrained habit of thought." If we keep learning a truth over and over again, we begin to think according to that truth.

I've been preaching for almost twenty years. When I sit in a Bible class or am reading the Bible at home, my thoughts about what I am reading automatically take the form of two or three key points of the text, usually with nice alliteration or grammatical parallelism. A passage speaks to me in the form of "Easy, Equitable, and Eternal" or "Love Lasts Longer than Loyalty." I admit, it's an occupational hazard, but it's also an ingrained habit of thought. I learned to think that way, and it helps me draw out and remember important truths—even when doing private devotional study.

As students of the Bible, each time we read about the Fool in Proverbs or the uncompromising Job or the penitent Zaccheus, our mind becomes a little more (or in the case of the Fool, a little less) like theirs. We begin to *see* hardship differently. We begin to *see* sin and greed differently. We begin to *see* the value of godly wisdom. Our thoughts are made new and, as a result, our lives are transformed.

Repetition often makes the second step, *concentration*, more difficult. The more times we've read a passage, the less we tend to concentrate on it. The exact opposite needs to

---

[8] Ibid., 64-66.

be true. Concentration is our investment of our entire being in what we are learning. We should take every fiber of our being, every thought, to the Scriptures. How else can we shine the light into our lives if we leave 90% of our being disengaged from the study?

The opposite is true as well. If we are only giving a passage 10% of our mind, we're going to miss 90% of what the passage is saying! When I see kids trying to do homework, watch television, tweet, post, upload, and sing along to their earbuds, I wonder how much is actually being retained. Some research says that for every "distraction" we lose 80% of our comprehension! That means when you open your Bible, you are at 100% potential. When you proceed to turn on a music c.d., you just dropped to 20% comprehension. When you set your cellphone next to you so you can text or socialize, you just dropped to 4%. If the t.v. is on, you are down to 0.8% comprehension! Throw a few kids into the mix and you have to resort to scientific notation!

Comprehension, the third step, moves the information from external fact to internal reality. In the field of education this is referred to as assimilation and accommodation.[9] What we read and observe is not only acknowledged as factual, it's incorporated into our view of reality. In other words, when we comprehend a truth, it changes the way we interpret the world from that day forward! How many of us study the Word of God with that goal in mind? Very few, unfortunately, strive for this change. However, it must be the goal of every study opportunity.

Foster's final point brings us back to our discussion of "light shining." *Reflection* helps us to determine the

---

[9] Jonathan Kim, "Intellectual Development and Christian Formation," in James Estep and Jonathan Kim, *Christian Formation: Integrating Theology & Human Development* (Nashville: B&H Academic, 2010), 64-68.

significance of what we have learned. When we first learn about the sacrifice of Christ on the cross, we appreciate it as an act of penal substitution—Jesus died so we don't have to. But that means the importance of the cross basically ends once we are saved. As we read about taking up our cross (Luke 9:23), we begin to "reflect" on the relationship between sacrifice and Christian living. We read further about obedience and the cross in Philippians 2:5-11. As we continue to comprehend more about the cross and reflect on its meaning for us as Christians, the significance of the cross to our life doesn't diminish after our conversion, it grows and informs everything we do—even our relationship with our spouses (Eph 5:25-33).

This four-step model is invaluable in shining the light of God's Word into every part of our life. We study repeatedly the truths of Scripture, apply our heart, mind, and soul to the Word and the Word to them, are transformed by our new thoughts, and consider daily the importance of each nugget of truth. This thorough and methodical approach assures us that no stone goes unturned in our search for truth and its application to our lives.

Personal Questions

1. How have you used the Bible like a solution manual instead of a textbook? Have you found it "insufficient" when used this way?

2. Of the four steps described by Foster, with which do you struggle the most? Do you have a systematic way of studying the Bible to take full advantage of each step?

3. Memorize John 1:1-5. Write your own "paraphrase" for the passage. A paraphrase is your understanding of the Scripture that roughly follows the line of thought of the Bible. *The Message* is a paraphrase of the Bible. Feel free to consult it for technique; however, DO NOT READ JOHN 1:1-5 from *The Message*. Let your paraphrase be your own.

Journal Reflections

1. In what ways do the Bible and prayer shine light on different areas of your life? Try to "shine the light of God" into dark corners of your life and see what you find. Are there areas of darkness that reject the understanding that the light brings?

2. During the next week, read through the book of Ephesians, one chapter each day. As you read, consider whether what you are reading describes your life. At some point throughout the week, compare a seemingly "unspiritual" decision to what you are learning from Ephesians. Consider the situation from every angle. How can you make it a "spiritual" decision?

MEDITATION

Opening Ourselves to God's Presence

R ichard Foster defines Christian mediation as "the ability to hear God's voice and obey his word."[10] For many of us, this definition sounds more like prayer than meditation. How might it be different?

The truth is that Foster is right on the mark. As we develop the discipline of meditation we improve our hearing and obeying. I don't know if I would call meditation an "ability," but it definitely "enables" better hearing and obeying. But as was mentioned before, the correlation between the discipline and the desired results is not always as simple as 1:1.

This point highlights the differences between the disciplines. As much as mediation may sound like it's the same as prayer, it's not. Prayer is communion with God. Meditation facilitates the communion experienced in prayer and through Bible study. As we will see soon, solitude creates "space" and "silence" for meditation, prayer, and study to occur.

Meditation that doesn't facilitate communion with God through prayer and Bible study would be more Eastern than Christian. Eastern meditation seeks to "empty" one's mind and "center" one's life on oneself. Christian meditation seeks

---

[10] Foster, *Celebration*, 17.

to fill one's mind with the things of God and "center" one's life in the middle of God's will. Yes, there is some emptying in this process, but it's with the *immediate goal* of refilling our minds with God!

We are warned in Matthew 12:43-45 that a life that has been cleansed but not filled with God will attract more demons afterwards than before the life was cleansed. The same could be true of meditation. If we attempt to empty our minds of worldly distractions and evil thoughts, but do not replace those thoughts with thoughts of God, we set ourselves up for failure. We should take this warning, if not literally, very seriously.

What is Meditation?

Few people doubt the need for meditation; the Psalms are filled with calls to meditate and descriptions of its blessings. Where people struggle is the biblical explanation of meditation. Is it to simply "dwell upon" something or to invest our entire conscience on something, which would make it similar to concentration? Or does it imply seeking a mystical "out of body" experience?

Peter's encounter with God in Acts 10 provides some insights into a biblical understanding. In 10:9-10, while praying, Peter "fell into a trance." The Greek word is *ekstasis* and literally means "change of place," or "change of state." The term was not uncommon in the first century, often referring to a divine revelation or out of body experience. As it was understood, one would "travel" to another place or state of being and gain some information from the deity or experience discovered there. It's easy to see why Luke's description of Peter's experience employs this term.

This story begs the question, should we attempt or expect the same thing? Should we hope to leave our bodies behind or experience some supernatural revelation or guidance for life? I'm going with the answer, "Yes."

Before you give up on me, let me explain what I mean. Say you are working diligently at your desk, confined on three and a half sides by your grey, carpeted cubicle. Your inbox is three times higher than your outbox. It's 11:30 a.m. and it feels like 11:30 p.m. You have a proposal to submit to your boss before you can leave for lunch—which you just found out about this morning! You are hungry, angry, lonely, and tired. You are on the brink. Then your wife calls to tell you she just ran into the garage door with the new-to-you 1999 Volvo you just bought her. At this point if you don't have an *ecstatic* experience, you won't have a wife or a car when you get home.

What do I mean?

If you reply to your wife based on the state, or *statis*, you are currently in, the remainder of your life, for as short as it may be, will not be pleasant. If, however, you reply *ekstatis*, you might have a chance. By not allowing your situation to determine what you think, say, and do, you will have officially had an ecstatic experience.

How does this help understand meditation?

People historically have made two mistakes in understanding meditation. Monks took the definition of "a change of place" too literally and found themselves holed up in a monastery trying to free themselves of the distractions of this world. Mystics took the definition too "spiritually" and attempted to reach some supernatural level of being, or "status." Both made use of techniques such as self-flagellation and starvation to help them escape the confines of the world around them.

Meditation is not that complicated. Meditation involves taking time to assess your situation from God's perspective. Instead of a bird's eye view of a situation, we need to get a God's eye view. We need to take a moment to step away from our life and appraise it spiritually. Remember one of our key verses, "But he who is spiritual appraises all things" (1 Cor 2:15). Christians get caught up in the flow of this world; we shouldn't. Meditation helps us to see the way God sees, hear the way he hears, and do what he would do.

Peter wasn't finished yet

Before we leave the story of Peter's vision, we need to look at one more piece of the puzzle. In Acts 10:19 we find Peter doing what most of us will readily recognize. He is "reflecting on the vision." Whether he was doing this while still entranced or immediately afterwards is not clear. Acts 10:17 says that he was greatly perplexed "in himself" (KJV and the Greek text). The vision was over, but the trance may not have been. In either case, Peter remained in a state of reflection on what he had seen.

Meditation is not meditation without reflection. While reflection is also a part of Bible study, part four to be exact, it's equally important in meditation. In meditation, prayer, and study we can learn a great deal from God, but we must spend time understanding what we have learned. I don't think Peter was perplexed by the content of the dream, strange though it was. I think he was perplexed by its apparent lack of meaning. Was God really worried about what Peter was and was not eating? Peter was trying to understand what God had revealed to him.

As a result of reflecting on the vision, Peter was ready when the men (Gentiles to be more specific) from Cornelius' house arrived. Because he connected the vision to real life, he invited them in, gave them lodging, and went with them the next morning. Don't forget that all three of those actions were basically against Jewish law! The point is that reflection is the internalization of what we learn from God during meditation, prayer, and study. We must make what we learn a part of the way that we think about life. Without reflection and internalization, we will continue to think and see the same way. Without that internal change, we will continue to respond to life as we always have, and that is not what God wants us to do.

Taking Stock

We've all been told at some point in our lives to "take stock of ourselves." What does that really mean? Basically, we need to know who we are and what we have. The Bible teaches just such a principle in Philippians 4:8 when Paul writes, "Finally, brethren, whatever is true, whatever is honorable, whatever is right, whatever is pure, whatever is lovely, whatever is of good repute, if there is any excellence and if anything worthy of praise, dwell on these things."

"Dwell" in this passage is not simply "thinking about constantly." The Greek word literally means "to take an account or inventory."[11] Paul is saying, "Take an inventory of these things and see if you find any of these virtuous characteristics present." Of course, the question is "present where?" I believe we are to take inventory of these qualities in our lives. What good does it do to look for these virtues in the world? Instead, we should be looking into our own lives to see if they are present.

---

[11] *Strong's Exhaustive Concordance: New American Standard Bible*, updated ed. (La Habra: Lockman Foundation, 1995), s.v. #3049.

Wow! That changes the meaning—and implications—of this passage quite a bit. It's one thing for God to want me to concentrate and meditate on virtuous and excellent qualities around me. It's another thing entirely if he expects me to actually find them in my own life. Yet, that is what the verse says.

Jesus basically gives this same instruction in Luke 14:28-31. If a man wants to build a tower, he makes sure he has enough resources. If a king is to enter battle, he assesses his troops. If we are going to live a Christian life, we need to know what talents, spiritual gifts, virtues, and strengths we have. We also need to know how to use them

Meditation provides the time and venue for this evaluation. Perhaps you are faced with a difficult decision about a personal relationship. In meditation, you consider how God has prepared you—to date—to tackle this difficulty. If the temptation is sexual, have you developed the purity needed to overcome it. If not, flee immorality! If you believe you have been tried and proved in that area, maybe it's okay to enter into a relationship.

At work you may face a challenge to your temper. A new co-worker continuously brags about his work and tends to take credit for the ideas of others. Do you have the peace of God present in your life that would allow you to interact with that person without losing your cool? If not, carefully consider what qualities you do have that might protect you from losing your self-control. Maybe you can be the peacemaker for other colleagues who are upset or the one who can praise God even when your idea is the one stolen.

The Process of Meditation

Given what we've considered, meditation involves three phases: (1) mentally stepping away from life, including ordinary circumstance and difficult situations, (2) reflecting on God and his word, and (3) taking an inventory of yourself. In any situation in life, these three actions will help you make decisions which are in accordance with God's will.

By stepping away from life in that moment, we avoid letting the situation dictate our response. Counting to ten when you are upset is similar; meditation is just more effective. You don't have to physically run off into a closet at work, but you do have to mentally "lay aside every encumbrance and the sin which so easily entangles us" (Heb 12:1).

After stepping away, we must consider what God would want us to do and how he would want us to do it. That means using what we've learned from the Bible and from our experience following him, called discernment, to assess the situation as spiritual beings. Reflection would also include prayer.

After taking the time to reflect on the situation, we need to see how God has prepared us to do his will. If God does not tempt us beyond what we can handle, then when trials, tribulations, and temptations come, the solution *must* be available within us! However, we must take inventory of our spiritual lives to find the "excellence" that God has developed in us for just this purpose.

We can't expect this process to be quick, which is probably why meditation usually brings to mind images of solitude. But we can expect to get better at it. As we mature our ability to assess and take captive every thought, we can step away quickly—and metaphorically, bring Scripture to bear on the issue, and know ourselves well enough to know the right course of action.

This view of meditation as an active process may be fairly new to you, but it's both Scriptural and practical. However, I don't want to diminish meditation as a time of extended prayer in the presence of God. As you will continue to see, disciplines reinforce each other. So meditation doesn't have to be just problem-focused. It can also be a time of personal assessment, of relationship-building with God, and of growth in God's Word.

Personal Practices

1. How would you describe meditation in a practical way? Don't forget the three phases.

2. Why is internalization an important final "step" in meditation?

3. Take an inventory of "excellence" in your life. How has God groomed you for discerning his will and handling difficulties?

David Srygley

Journal Reflections

1. Choose your favorite Bible passage and meditate on that passage each day. Record the ways in which it directs your mind towards God. In what ways does the passage and meditation direct your heart toward obeying God's Word?

2. Think about a decision you need to make. Instead of making a list of pros and cons, write about how the decision will affect your relationship with God. Will it bring glory to God? Will it strengthen your relationship? Will it add to your inventory more purity, justice, righteousness?

FASTING

Desiring God and His Will Before Everything Else.

Our list of "things I can't live without" continues to grow longer. My kids tell me they can't live without their cell phones, laptop computers, cars, cable television, and game consoles. At the bottom of their list is food, clothes, jobs, etc. Oddly enough, the list is very upside down. At the top of the list are the things they need to be satisfied and at the bottom are the things needed to survive!

In society today, most people feel they deserve more than just the basics of life. Perhaps they are right! Jesus did, after all, promise us an abundant life. So maybe if Jesus gave us all game consoles, cell phones, better jobs, *et cetera*, we would be happier—and he would have made good on his promise.

But we know that stuff doesn't make us happy. Why do people who have so much stuff always want more? It's not because the stuff they have accumulated brings them so much contentment; it's because it doesn't. They want more because the abundance they do have isn't making them happy at all.

So, if more is less; is less more? Will having less stuff make us happier than having more stuff? Nope. That won't work either. Martyrdom is a great idea but isn't for all of us. Saying that a poor Christians makes a good Christian puts as much emphasis on money as the source or measure of Christianity as those who say rich Christians are blessed Christians. Money and stuff aren't what it's about. The center of Christian fulfillment is contentment with God.

Satisfaction can only come from God, a point Paul drives home in Philippians 4:11, 13, "Not that I speak from want; for I have learned to be content in whatever circumstances I am... I can do all things through Him who strengthens me." We say it with our lips, but our lives are filled with so much stuff that you'd never know we knew it! That being the case, does that mean we don't really believe it? If we believed it, we wouldn't be accumulating new toys at every opportunity. If we believed it, we would be depending on God for contentment instead of more stuff. Ironically then, more is more! More faith in God's provision is more abundance of life.

This recognition is where fasting comes in. Fasting teaches us that satisfaction—even physical satisfaction—comes from God. When we start stripping away other ways of meeting our needs, we soon find what really matters. Fasting helps accomplish that goal.

Normally we strip away the easy things first: no more ice cream or no more snacks between meals. Then we move towards the more difficult: no more cable television or no more sleeping through church. Finally we make it to the impossible: no more drinking or smoking or no more working on the weekends. As we eliminate these "vices" we begin to feel more dependent on God for satisfaction. Unfortunately, after the first couple of sacrifices, the going gets tough. We need some encouragement along the way.

Fasting provides encouragement by letting us see the power of God working in our lives. When done for the right reasons, fasting shows us how substantive God's power is. His power sustains us and strengthens us and even uplifts us. When our bodies *should* be giving out on us, we find that

God's strength endures. This doesn't mean it will be easy; it will just be powerful.

Fasting as Desire for God

Earlier when I said, "for the right reasons," what did I mean? The Bible teaches at least two important facts about fasting, even though it gives very little instructions on it. First, fasting must be driven by a desire for God. Fasting for health benefits is counter-productive to spiritual growth. If you want to diet, do so, but don't call it fasting. If we fast with the ulterior motive of weight loss, or worse the primary motive of weight loss, then we have violated the most important teaching of all. Fasting is about desiring God, not about desiring better health, better bodies, or longer lives.

I should make one side point about "weight loss." If food has become your god, and it's evident by your weight, then weight loss still isn't your goal. Your goal should be putting God first as the one true God. This reprioritization will certainly result in weight loss, but the change is a result of putting God above food. If, however, laziness or other addictions have become your god, resulting in weight problems or not, then fasting is still appropriate for you for the same reasons. You need to learn to desire God.

Jesus tells the disciples of John that the disciples of Jesus did not need to fast while Jesus was still present on earth. "But the days will come," Jesus continues, "when the bridegroom is taken away from them, and then they will fast" (Matt 9:15). Why would they fast after Jesus ascends? Though there is ample discussion on the subject, I believe it's because they will have an overwhelming desire for him. God incarnate who walked among them is now gone, and they will fast as they await his return. Fasting shows a desire for God's presence in our lives.

Jesus' answer to John's disciples comes on the heels of his Sermon on the Mount. In these teachings Jesus said, "Blessed are those who hunger and thirst for righteousness, for they shall be satisfied" (Matt 5:6). If Jesus has his teachings on the Mount in mind when he answers John's disciples, then fasting is hungering and thirsting for righteousness. If that is the case, the disciples of Jesus didn't fast because they weren't "hungering and thirsting." They were instead feeding daily on the righteousness and presence of God among them. You don't have to hunger and thirst when you are sitting at a banquet table—unless of course you choose to!

One other teaching in Matthew's gospel reinforces the idea that fasting is a part of our desire and reliance on God. In Matthew 4:4 Jesus states that "Man shall not live on bread alone, but on every word that proceeds out of the mouth of God." This statement is made to the Devil when he tries to tempt Jesus to turn stone to bread after Jesus had been fasting for forty days. Though Jesus was hungry, his desire to please God and his trust in God's provision outweighed his current condition and needs, even though the desire for physical food may have been overwhelming after forty days.

Fasting as Focus on Others

The second teaching regarding fasting is actually more of a warning. Both Jesus, in the Sermon on the Mount, and the prophet Isaiah confront the people of Israel about their fasts. We are probably most familiar with Jesus' statement, "And whenever you fast, do not put on a gloomy face as the hypocrites do, for they neglect their appearance in order to be seen fasting by men. Truly I say to you, they have their reward in full" (Matt 6:16). He goes on to say that Christians should fast in such a way that men will not know they are fasting. By fasting with humility they receive blessings from God.

While the first teachings remind us that fasting is about desiring God, the second serves to warn us not to focus on ourselves. The worst case scenario is self-aggrandizement. Not only am I focused on me, I want others to focus on me also. I want the accolades of men.

However, most Christians are not as pharisaical as, say, the Pharisees. We don't flaunt our righteousness before men. We just flaunt it before ourselves in our own minds. We roll over our self-righteousness again and again in our mind. We consider our humility and self-sacrifice. We build for ourselves a spiritual "bed of ashes and sackcloth" on which to lie. Privately, we feel pretty good about our righteousness.

Isaiah, predating Jesus by a few hundred years, warned Israel of misusing their fasts as well. The thoughts of Jesus and Isaiah are remarkably similar: "Is it a fast like this which I choose, a day for a man to humble himself? Is it for bowing one's head like a reed, and for spreading out sackcloth and ashes as a bed? Will you call this a fast, even an acceptable day to the Lord" (Isa 58:5)? The grammar in the final question implies that the expected answer is, "NO!" Just like Jesus, Isaiah warns the people that God isn't happy with their "humility."

So what was God's solution to Israel's false humility? Isaiah continues,

> Is this not the fast which I choose, to loosen
> the bonds of wickedness, to undo the bands
> of the yoke, and to let the oppressed go free,
> and break every yoke? Is it not to divide your
> bread with the hungry, and bring the homeless
> poor into the house; when you see the naked,

to cover him; and not to hide yourself from
your own flesh? (Isa 58:6-7)

The solution to being focused on ourselves appears to be
focusing on others during our time of fasting! But how can
our focus be both on God and on others? Remember, I didn't
say that the first teaching was to *focus* on God; I said it's that
we must desire God and his presence. Stated another way,
the motivation for fasting is a desire to be in the presence of
God. This second teaching, or warning, is that the fail-safe
for not making fasting "about me" is to focus our thoughts
and minds on the needs of others. Listen to what Isaiah says
will happen when we desire God and focus on others:

> And the Lord will continually guide you, and
> satisfy your desire in scorched places, and give
> strength to your bones; and you will be like
> a watered garden, and like a spring of water
> whose waters do not fail. (Isa 58:11)

If we desire to experience the presence of God, to be
strengthened by his mighty power, and to be filled with
eternal water, we must put the needs of others, not just before
our own, but in place of our own! Fasting teaches us to do
exactly that.

The Fast

If there is a spiritual discipline that has been written on
ad infinitum, it's fasting. Though out of vogue for some
time among Christians, and especially evangelicals, men like
Richard Foster, Franklin Graham, and Donald Whitney have
helped to reestablish the practice as not only acceptable, but

important. For this reason, it's not necessary to provide an elaborate set of instructions. There are plenty of books on the topic. For our purposes, let me summarize in a couple of steps the usual procedures.

1. Start with a simple, partial 24-hour fast. A partial fast allows you to drink clear juices as necessary to stave off hunger. Use a partial fast the first few times.
2. After a few partial fasts, attempt a 24-hour fast with nothing but water to drink. However, drink plenty of water.
3. After a couple of successful 24-hour fasts, get a book on the topic and keep up the good work!

With that said, let me back up. You don't need to aim for 24 hours the first few times. In fact, let me discourage you from doing so! Why? I don't want your fast to become about *your* victory—or we're right back to violating all the teachings we've discussed. I do want you to experience a sense of victory, but not in the pat-myself-on-the-back way. I want you to experience the victory God has in store for you when you let his strength become your strength in the accomplishment of his will.

Instead, I want you to start really small. Try a one-hour, totally sold-out fast. By that I mean take one hour when you would normally be eating and give it to God through service to another. Maybe on your lunch break you can run over to a local soup kitchen and serve meals. Maybe instead of dinner one night you meet with a friend or neighbor to talk about God's work in your life or their need for God in their own. In both cases, politely decline anything other than water.

Why do I suggest this as a starting point? I believe that most people who fast focus too much on the fast. Like every spiritual discipline, it's a tool to accomplish a specific purpose. Too much focus on the tool can have very undesirable outcomes; ask anyone who keeps his eye on the hammer instead of the nail! The purpose of fasting isn't to go hungry. The purpose is to let God be your strength. This purpose is enhanced, and your soul guarded, by relying on God for strength *while* serving others. This accommodation of fasting seems to be what God had in mind when he spoke through Isaiah.

Part of the New Paradigm

Reenvisioning fasting as a way of becoming dependent on God to accomplish his will is part of our new paradigm for spiritual disciplines. Fasting in this sense isn't a form of monastic self-degradation. Neither is it a mystic's method for subduing the physical so that the soul can be set free. Fasting, in our new way of thinking, teaches us that God's strength is sufficient for all his purposes.

Both halves of this statement are critical for the proper utilization of fasting as a spiritual discipline. For centuries fasting has taught Christians to rely on God's strength. Indeed, we need to know that God's grace and strength are sufficient. Unfortunately, most Christians used fasting to strengthen themselves for their own benefit. These benefits may have included some very spiritual goals, but the practitioner was still focused on, in some sense, becoming stronger for their own sake.

Isaiah is very clear that fasting must have a purpose other than simply learning to depend on God. That other purpose is seen in our extended definition. The purpose of fasting is teaching us to depend on God's strength to accomplish God wills. If we just want to become "more spiritual" through fasting, we are erring as the monks did who disengaged from the world and worldly things, such as food, but for no useful purpose! What good does it do us, or God for that matter, if we learn to be dependent on God's strength—but have no intention of fulfilling God's purpose for our lives! Why would God strengthen a workman who has no desire to serve him? (Notice how this takes us back to the desire for God to be our motivation!)

The practice of fasting, as I've outlined, brings together both the need to learn dependence on God's strength and the purpose for learning dependence on God's strength. If we don't desire God and his will then fasting is merely dieting—and a bad way of dieting at that. But if, by fasting, we discover that we can accomplish God's will without any resources or strength of our own, imagine how excuses and doubts will melt away. No longer will our lives be filled with, "Not me, Lord" and "I can't do that." Instead, we will boldly proclaim, just as Paul did two thousand years ago, "I can do all things through him who strengthens me" (Phil 4:13).

Personal Practices

1. How is fasting like "hungering and thirsting after righteousness"?

2. Describe fasting as a tool for learning to depend on God to do God's work. (Refer to Isaiah 58.)

3. This might be one of the most difficult disciplines to practice. First, identify an opportunity to serve God by serving others. Second, try to work out with whoever is involved a time to serve that would normally have been a mealtime for you. Finally, make it happen. Usually people use their time fasting for prayer and Bible reading. You'll need to do that to get ready for your service. In the time leading up to your time of service, read as much as you can of the Letter to the Philippians. Include prayer throughout the reading and as you are serving.

Journal Reflections

1. Have you ever thought about why you desire to grow spiritually and/or become more dependent on God? Have your goals for spiritual growth and strengthening changed as you consider the purpose of fasting?

2. What areas of your life or things in your life do you honestly feel provide you more satisfaction than God? Remember, the answers could include family, leisure, work, etc. How might fasting help you learn to surrender those desires to God?

SIMPLICITY

*Our preparation for service and
life in God's Kingdom!*

Foster states, "The Christian Discipline of simplicity is an inward reality that results in an outward life-style."[12] Credit cards provide an excellent example of this truth. I know lots of people who take out debt consolidation loans in order to pay off credit card debt. They simplify their payments, save money on interest, and usually pay off the loans faster than they could've paid off their cards. This process exemplifies an outward change of lifestyle. Unfortunately, most of those people have their credit cards maxed out again within a few years! Now they have both a loan payment and credit card payments. What went wrong?

The obvious answer is that they didn't cut up their cards. Of course, it's very easy to request, and the credit company is more than willing to provide, replacement cards. So it's not the cards' fault.

The deeper problem lies within the heart. If you consolidate your debt—the debt you accumulated because you overspent—but don't change your spending habits, you are right back to square one. And spending habits are related to heart habits. In order to prevent overspending again, you

---

[12] Foster, *Celebration*, 81.

have to change your desires. If you still desire newer cars, fancier clothes, latest electronics, more channels, and faster internet, your spending habits will never change—you will forever live in debt! First you have to change what your heart desires, then your life will change.

Speed Trap Ahead

Many small towns in Texas make a large portion of their revenues from speeding tickets. One such town sits on my family's routine travel route to see grandparents. Just beyond a blind curve surrounded by dense pine trees is a twenty mile per hour drop in speed. For a city needing revenue, this arrangement is ideal. Luckily, a very helpful and compassionate family put up a large sign in their front yard that reads, "Speed Trap Ahead!"

The Bible is replete with such signs. Two types of warnings in particular should give us pause. The first warning, from Jesus' teachings on the Sermon on the Mount, reminds us of the pitfalls of wealth. Jesus first warns,

> Do not lay up for yourselves treasures upon earth, where moth and rust destroy and where thieves break in and steal. But lay up for yourselves treasures in heaven, where neither moth nor rust destroys, and where thieves do not break in or steal; for where your treasure is, there will your heart be also. (Matt 6:19-21)

We often brag that we won't let our ambition and desire for more interfere with our living for Christ. Jesus says it will. So who should you believe, your own rationalization or the words of God? Christians take this admonition entirely too lightly. We play the "yeah, but" trump card when people, even Jesus, start talking about becoming trapped by our wealth. And in case you think being poor or middle class automatically prevents you from falling prey to wealth, remember it's not the possession and money that is the sin, it's the love of money (1 Tim 6:10). Many people who get by on modest incomes have unhealthy desires for more.

Jesus further illuminates the core problem when he says, "[F]or either he will hate the one and love the other, or he will hold to one and despise the other" (Matt 6:24). It's a choice. Do we want to give our whole heart to God or turn it over to the world? Again, we can argue, "There's no way that I would let money or possessions get between me and God." However, this statement assumes you get to determine whether God feels unloved by you. If *he* says that the pursuit of wealth means you don't love him, then how can we argue.

The second warning is a bit more subtle but equally dangerous. The apostle John warns that loving the world will result in our destruction. In 1 John 2:15-17, he writes:

> Do not love the world, nor the things in the world. If anyone loves the world, the love of the Father is not in him. For all that is in the world, the lust of the flesh and the lust of the eyes and the boastful pride of life, is not from the Father, but is from the world. And the world is passing away, and also its lusts; but the one who does the will of God abides forever.

In the final sentence, John makes a dire prediction for those who desire the things of this world; they will pass away with it. But, he says, "the one who does the will of God" will live forever. This passage is full of subtleties. If you desire the world, when the world is destroyed, you will be destroyed with it. How do you know if you desire God and not the world? You do his will. Those who love God do his will! If you love the world and the things of this world, when the time comes to obey God at the cost of personal gain you simply will not do it. But if you love God exclusively, then obeying his will is easy.

God-Centered Life.[13]

When our life revolves around our world it can't revolve around God. When God is not the center of our life we can expect to grow cold in our love for him and in our desire to serve him. The discipline of simplicity keeps the world from becoming the center of our life. Of course, just like fasting, if we don't desire God then we will not desire to have him at the center of our lives.

Many writers have pointed out that in his Model Prayer in Matthew 6:9-13 Jesus doesn't ask much from God. It begins with an attitude of praise and submission and then moves to three simple requests: daily bread, forgiveness of sins, and guidance. The last two are as God-centered as the first two. Only daily bread is requested on our own behalf. Could it be that the laundry list of needs that we take to the Father actually detracts from what is really important in prayer—God's will? What if we prayed, "Give us this day only what we need for today to sustain us"? Doesn't sound all that different than the manna God provided in the wilderness. How would that change in our prayers change both what we think we need and how we appear to God? Suddenly,

---

[13] Willard, *Spirit*, 168. Willard refers to this as staying "within the bounds" of God's order. Estes identifies this principle in the "values" found in Old Testament Wisdom Literature in Estes, 62.

we are focusing on God's will and his provision and not on our own needs. (Remember, we learned this principle in our lesson on prayer.)

Simplifying our lives and our requests also demonstrates trust in God. Jesus encouraged his hearers in Matthew 6:25-34 to rely on God's perfect provision. He describes the consistent provision of God for the birds. They do not sow, harvest, or store away excess food, yet they always have enough to survive. If God values us more than the animals of the field, then why wouldn't he be just as kind to us? We can always depend on God to provide.

We learn another aspect of God's provision from this story as well. Birds take what they get. With some effort we can accept that God will always provide our needs so we shouldn't get exorbitant in our requests. But birds actually make no requests of God!

I know we are told to pray for "our daily bread," so I don't mean don't pray. However, most of our prayers probably resemble this: "Give us this day our daily bread. Make it a whole wheat ciabatta roll with sesame seeds. Maybe a light coating of warm olive oil served with roasted garlic in a balsamic vinegar dipping sauce—Lord willing!" Instead, if we desire a simple life, we should pray, "Give us this day our daily bread. Any bread is fine, Lord. Whatever you see fit. Amen."

This brings us an important note about Matthew 6:26. Jesus does not say that because we are worth more than the animals we will get more than the animals. His point is that since God loves us more than animals he would never provide for them and not provide for us! Too often this passage is used to say that our blessings will be proportionally larger because God loves us more. The Scripture only says that his love is a guarantee of constant provision.

As Jesus concludes this portion of his teaching, we learn that we are to seek the kingdom of God and his righteousness. If we do so, God will provide for our needs. But seeking his kingdom and his righteousness means lots of worldly desires will have to be sacrificed. Most of us are not willing to give up the things of this world for the kingdom of God—with the result that we wind up having to do everything for ourselves.

Doesn't God Want Me to Be Happy?

God wants you to be blessed, content, joyous, empowered, thankful, and a host of other positive feelings. Without getting into the theological debate about the difference between having joy and being happy, I'll even say that he wants you to be happy. But above happy, blessed, content, joyous, empowered, and thankful, he wants you to be ready!

Simplicity prepares us to serve God. When a villager hastily volunteers to follow Jesus, Jesus replies, "The foxes have holes, and the birds of the air have nests; but the Son of Man has nowhere to lay His head" (Matt 8:20). Disciples of Jesus are challenged to live without many of the conveniences of this worldly life. We still see this truth in the lives of missionaries in many countries—and even in some parts of America. If we have already simplified our lives, the obstacles to serving Jesus are already gone!

In Luke 14:16-24 Jesus tells a parable of people more concerned about their worldly life and possessions than enjoying the banquet offered by a benevolent man. One man had purchased property. Another had bought oxen. A third had just gotten married. This last excuse we may have issues with, but if the subject is simplicity, no one can argue that the single life is *simpler* than the married life. I am not, however, recommending you simplify your life by getting rid of your wife. The point of the story and all three of the excuses is that when we are entangled in the affairs and desires of this world, we will not be ready when we are called by God—into service or into his blessings. (Paul warns Timothy similarly in 2 Timothy 2:4.)

As the parable continues, who comes to the feast? The house is filled with the poor, lame, blind, and crippled. Did these people love food more than the first group? Did they love the benevolent man more than the first group? Likely, they didn't even know him. The truth is that they had no reason to say, "No," and all the reasons in the world to say, "Yes." While most of us recognize that we have all the reason in the world to say, "Yes," to the calling of God, we have more reasons in our lives to say, "No."

Taking Every Thought Captive

Like fasting, simplicity is about desiring God and depending on him. Where fasting emphasizes strength and dependence, simplicity emphasizes purity and devotion. Fasting teaches us that "I can do all things through him who strengthens me" (Phil 4:13). Simplicity teaches us that God's provision is perfect—he is all we need.

As Foster pointed out at the beginning of our study, simplicity begins on the inside. It's a decision that God is all we need. It's a decision that we can be no happier than when we are living fully in his will. It's a decision, not to accept what God provides, but to rejoice in what he provides.

Once we've made the decision to celebrate the life that God has planned for us, we can take the first step. We can decide that we will stop pursuing and accumulating worldly materials. From there we can begin to disencumber and disentangle our lives from the choking weeds of the worldly possessions we already have. Soon we can live free of the destruction, both eternal and temporal, that the addiction to the world brings.

Simplicity also provides a unique way to take thoughts captive. Simplicity allows us to take back our thoughts from the captivity of this world. A Chinese proverb often used in substance abuse counseling says, "First the man takes the drink, then the drink takes a drink, and then the drink takes the man." The same can be said about possessions, "First the man gets the world, then the world gets more world, and then world gets the man." Christians obsessed with worldly gain do not own their own thoughts; the world does.

By eliminating the things in our lives that keep our thoughts focused on this world, we can once again see and assess the world without bias. Like the poor and needy on the roadsides in Jesus' parable, what we know to be best is clear. If our lives are filled with desire for the world, we evaluate each life situation for its contribution to our desires. Simplicity prevents us from assessing situations for their benefit to us because we don't need anything. Christians living a simple life benefit from an unencumbered relationship with God. In other words, the truth has set them free!

Personal Practice

1. How is the simple life exemplified in the Model Prayer? Does your life resemble the life prayed for in the Model Prayer?

2. What benefits could you realize by simplifying your own life?

3. Choose one item in your house, at your work, or in your life to discard. Try to identify something that would prevent you from obeying God's will at the drop of a hat. As you do so, treat the process as a sacrifice to God. You can even imagine it's like an Old Testament freewill (wave) offering to God.

Journal Reflections

1. In what areas of your life do you need to confess a love of the things of this world?

2. What stuff in your life interferes with God fully directing your life? Where do you love or trust the world more than God? To help answer these questions, take an inventory of your bedroom and/or living room. As you write down each item, ask yourself what purpose the item serves in your life.

SOLITUDE AND SILENCE

*Removal of worldly "noise" to boldly
allow God to enter our being.*

The lesson on simplicity taught us to purge our lives of stuff and disentangle ourselves from the lusts of the world. The Christian discipline of simplicity, like fasting and meditation, encourages Christians to clear their lives of thoughts and desires that are spiritually unhealthy and hinder our obedience to Christ. As we wrap up our sixth and final discipline of preparation, we must clear one more obstacle from our lives—noise!

"TIME OUT!"

How many times have you wanted to scream that at the top of your lungs? Not at a soccer match, but in life. No matter what seems to be going on in our lives, more is always coming at us. Sometimes we just want everything to stop and let us get a handle on our thoughts and lives. The discipline of solitude and silence provides that spiritual time-out that we desire.

Jesus on multiple occasions had to escape from the press and noise of the crowds. In John 6:15 the Bible says the crowds were pressing in on him and trying to take him by force to be their king. (They had the right idea but the wrong approach.) So when we feel overwhelmed, even by the legitimate demands of our Christian life, and need a break, we can take comfort in knowing that the Son of God did too.

While it's easy for most of us to spot the "outside" noise in our lives, televisions, cell phones, irate bosses, raging drivers, etc., we often fail to recognize the "inside" noise. The inside noise is static in our own heads, or an interference with our ability or desire to hear God's voice. This interference comes in three forms, intellectual, worldly, and religious.

The Teacher in Ecclesiastes refers to intellectual noise when he states, "God made men plain, but they have engaged in too much reasoning" (Eccl 7:29, Jewish Publication Society Bible). Mankind's desire to know and understand everything creates lots of static. God already warned us that we cannot understand all his ways and thoughts (Isaiah 55:8), but we're determined to try anyways. We read articles, peruse books, view videos, and listen to talk shows trying to find answers. Instead, following the advice of the Teacher, we should accept that we are plain, or simple, people and are only meant to understand with clarity what God has revealed. The promise of God, in the remainder of the passage in Isaiah 55, is that what God has revealed is sufficient, "accomplishing what I desire, and ... succeeding in the matter for which I sent it" (Isa 55:11). If we can train ourselves to accept this truth, our lives will glisten with clarity.

Worldly noise inside our heads is a result of how we engage our brains. Too often we are engaged in talk that is both worldly and empty. Not only is it unproductive, it's destructive. Paul warns, "But avoid worldly and empty chatter, for it will lead to further ungodliness" (2 Tim 2:16). When we allow our heads to be filled with worldly noise, the message of God cannot penetrate.

By now you may have already remembered the third, and much more famous, "noise." In 1 Corinthians 13:1 Paul says, "If I speak with the tongues of men and of angels, but do not have love, I have become a noisy gong or a clanging cymbal." Even religious talk can become nothing but religious noise if it's not spoken in love. Engaging in loveless religious banter and debate, for that is what it will clearly devolve into, creates so much noise in our own heads and in the environment around us that neither we nor those around us can hear the voice of God.

Clearing Our Heads

The question may arise in some of your minds, "Can't God's message cut through all that noise? After all, he is God, and the Bible says his word is sharper than a two-edged sword!" This question reminds me a bit of the one, "Can God make a rock so big he couldn't pick it up?" The answer is the same. "Why would he bother?" God wants to be heard, but he wants you to want to hear him. Repeatedly, the Bible says, "He who has ears let him hear." God is speaking, but will we apply ourselves to hearing?

When we think about God speaking in the Old Testament, our minds almost always jump to Mt. Sinai (Exodus 19:18-19). God's presence surrounds the mountain with terrifying fire and black smoke. He speaks in the thunder. The earth quakes at his every word. And while we envision this event correctly, we forget that God usually preferred a more subtle approach. When God met with Elijah, he did so in the "gentle breeze" (1 King 19:11-12). When God called Samuel, he did so in the stillness of the night (1 Samuel 3). God met Moses in the lonely desert (Exodus 3). When God walked among his people, he did so as a servant (Philippians 2:5-8).

If God's *modus operandi* is speaking quietly, he doesn't have a chance of communicating with us in our busy, noisy lives. Or at least we don't have a chance of hearing him when he tries to talk with us. For all of the times you've said, "I just don't think God is calling me to this or that," could it be that he was calling, but your life was too noisy to hear him?

Fortress of Solitude

Some of you won't need an explanation, but for the rest, allow me to do so. In the great wisdom of Jor-El, Superman's biological father on Krypton, he sent his son to earth with a piece Kryptonian sunstone.[14] This stone, or crystal, was used to create the Fortress of Solitude. Here, Superman is able to retreat when needed. The Fortress plays a prominent role in many of the Superman movies.

Jesus, though lacking a Fortress, frequently sought out a place of solitude. Oddly enough, Jesus' purpose in seeking solitude is remarkably similar to Superman's. Both escaped into solitude for direction, strength, and comfort.

The longest period of solitude for Jesus recorded in the Bible is his forty day fast at the beginning of his ministry. In Matthew 4:1-2, Matthew writes, "Then Jesus was led up by the Spirit into the wilderness to be tempted by the devil. And after He had fasted forty days and forty nights, He then became hungry." This event takes place after Jesus' baptism and prior to the beginning of his ministry. Though the Bible

---

[14] The first Fortress of Solitude appears in "The Super-Key to Fort Superman" (Action Comics #241, June 1958). There are several revisions to the story of the Fortress of Solitude. In fact, it began before 1958 under a different name! I've chosen the one that best fits my purpose. I offer my apologies to Superman *connoisseurs* who likely understand the concept much better than I.

says he was led into the wilderness "to be tempted by the devil," the temptation came at the end of the time of solitude. The time in the wilderness appears to be a time of preparation for life and ministry through communion with God.

During our times of silence and solitude we are perfectly positioned to commune with God. This communion provides clarity to our mission and purpose, a sense of direction for our calling and ministry, and an affirmation of God's Word in our lives. Without clearing our heads and receiving the thoughts of God as our own, we will wander aimlessly through life.

As we learned from fasting, communion with God is a source of strength. Solitude reinforces this strength, especially spiritually. When Jesus was preparing himself to go to the cross, he sought solitude in the Garden of Gethsemane for clarity and to fortify his resolve (Matthew 26:36-46). Noise distracts, desensitizes, and dulls the senses. Silence and solitude sharpen our minds and spirits for purposeful service to God.

When we have too much noise in our lives, we are like the small child receiving instructions from his parent. When the T.V. is off, the radio or music player muted, and the child is focused on the parent, he has a MUCH better chance of obeying his parent. Because other noises aren't vying for his attention, he takes every thought captive for the purpose of obedience! If this situation is true for a child in the world, shouldn't it be true for a child of God?

Another reason Jesus apparently sought solitude was to deal with life. After Matthew records the story of John the Baptizer's death, he writes "Now when Jesus heard it, He withdrew from there in a boat, to a lonely place by Himself" (Matt 14:13). Jesus must have needed some time to sort out his feelings! Noise of all kinds can prevent us from effectively dealing with our emotions and struggles.

I often tell people who are grieving that they will want to tell the world, "Stop and let me off!" Too many feelings and not enough time or "quietness" to sort them out—or let them out. The world's irrational and clinical fear of being alone or being bored has robbed humans of the very thing they desperately need to cope with life—silence and solitude.

Greased Pigs!

When I was a freshman in college, I tried to catch a greased pig in a sea of mud. All I got out of the contest was a trip to the doctor and patch over one eye for two weeks. It wasn't as fun as it appears on television; few things are! But I learned an important lesson. It's hard to get a grip on something covered in oil that is wallowing around in water. Oil and water are natural enemies!

When trying to take our thoughts captive for obedience to Christ, the world is not going to make it easy. Just like the pig was better acculturated to the mud, our thoughts are, in the beginning, more in tune with the world. When the pig is running around in the mud, it's hard to catch because it's at home there. But if it were me and the pig in a small, dry, clean pigpen by ourselves, I might stand a better chance. So it is with taking thoughts captive for Christ. If I take my thoughts out of the muddy mess of the world and try to understand them apart from their worldly environment, I can see them in a different light—the light of God's word and presence.

Conclusion

Silence and solitude are two sides of the same coin, and the coin is called disengagement. Now I know I said that a good model for spiritual disciplines is one that helps you engage the world, but silence and solitude are the caveat. Before we can use our faith to engage the world, we have to make sure that our faith is pure, holy, and blameless. We need to carefully examine the decision that we are going to make by faith. We need to ask, "Am I hearing God?" "Am I being influenced by the world?" "Am I assessing this thought spiritually?" We can ask these questions and assess our lives better in the cleft of the Rock.

When faced with challenges, especially the unrelenting, unyielding demands on our life, resources, and walk with God, take a time out. Spend some precious time with the Creator in careful reflection. And here's some advice. Start BIG! It's actually easier to step away from life for this time of rejuvenation and reflection when the decision being considered is big. I'm not saying the decision is necessarily easier; I'm saying the recognition of the value of stepping away is easier. Bigger problems are easier to assess. We're able to see the many facets of the problem and the many ways in which God addresses the situation in his word when the decision is big.

Over time, we become so comfortable taking that time out and reflecting on our decisions that we do it with any situation or problem, no matter what the size. We get so good at making those decisions that all we need is a telephone booth and a split second of solitude, and we are ready to take on the world. As our knowledge of God's Word grows, we see ways to apply it in our everyday life. As we mature, we become experts at the application of our faith and knowledge of God to every thought and every decision, and that is what spiritual disciplines are all about.

Personal Practices

1. Make a list of "inside" noise and "outside" noise that interferes with hearing God.

2. What are the benefits of turning off the noise? What can we gain from silence and solitude?

3. Before you answer a question or respond to another person, pause and pray for wisdom. If what you want to say sounds like empty chatter, ask for a moment to find a quiet place and pray, and then respond.

Journal Reflections

1. Fast from noise this week. Choose something that you know inhibits your ability to hear God's voice and discern his will and set it aside. Remember, don't look for something bad to get rid of; most of our lives are overfilled with good, not evil. Journal new thoughts you encounter as you free up your attention and turn it to God.

2. Record each wanton or meaningless word you use throughout the day. Consider how practicing solitude and silence might have changed the way you spoke. If there is a particular person or situation creating noise, how might you withdraw to seek God?

SUBMISSION

Freedom from the Need to Have Our Own Way!

With the discipline of submission we come to our first Discipline of Engagement. The first six disciplines are to help us prepare for engaging the world; now we turn to actually engaging it! However, we cannot engage the world without first understanding our place in the grand scheme of life on this earth. The discipline of submission, literally, "puts us in our place."

Many people have the wrong idea of submission. It's not doing whatever anyone tells you to do. If this were the case, we'd be in a state of constant ethical conflict. Do I have to do something I'm told to do if I think it's wrong?

Instead, submission is the practice of placing others' needs before your own. More importantly, it's the attitude that others' needs are more important than your own (Philippians 2:1-4). Like simplicity, we must begin with a change of heart. When we begin loving people more than we love ourselves, submission becomes almost automatic in our lives.

Heart of Submission

Consider Paul's command to spouses in Ephesians 5:21-33. Ephesians 5:21 says to "be subject to one another in the fear of Christ." He then goes on to tell wives to be subject to their husbands. While it must be acknowledged that "be subject" is not in the sentence in the Greek; no verb is present. As a result, you have two options. First is to supply a form of "to be," making the sentence read, "Wives, *be* to your own husbands." With this construction you would need a referent, or a previous "to be" verb to give meaning to the "be." That referent is "be subject in the previous verse. The second option is to import the immediately preceding verb into the sentence. In this case, that would be "be subject." So you have two options, but both result in the same translation!

After telling the wives "to be subject" to their husbands, Paul tells the husbands to love their wives sacrificially, just as Christ loved the church. Why would he tell the husbands to sacrificially love their wives unless, in his understanding, sacrificial love is either the fulfillment of or the foundation for mutual submission! Given the context of the command, both are likely true.

In his letter to the Philippian church, Paul argues for an attitude of submission from the same starting point: love, fellowship, affection, and compassion. He writes:

> Therefore if there is any encouragement in Christ, if there is any consolation of love, if there is any fellowship of the Spirit, if any affection and compassion, make my joy complete by being of the same mind, maintaining the same love, united in spirit, intent on one purpose. Do nothing from selfishness or empty conceit, but with humility of mind regard one another as more important than yourselves" (Phil 2:1-3).

Before you can begin to regard others as more important than yourself, you must possess the Spirit and allow him to infect the way you think and feel about others. Again, we find ourselves returning to the core premise that spiritual disciplines train us "to take every thought captive to the obedience of Christ" (2 Cor 10:5), even thoughts about one another!

Head of Submission

If the heart of submission is love, the head of submission is self-denial. Self-denial is a conscious choice. We don't accidentally submit to another person. We may accidentally do something that benefits another, but that's not submission; that's serendipity. That action may even cost us something, but that's not sacrifice. We must decide to submit, which is why it's in the imperative form; it's a command to be obeyed.

Paul demonstrates this choice for us. In 1 Corinthians 9:19, he writes, "For though I am free from all men, I have made myself a slave to all, that I might win the more." Notice, Paul says he has made himself a slave. God didn't make him a slave. No lord or master made him a slave. No one bought him or sold him. He chose to become a slave of his own free will.

Hands of Submission

This decision of Christ leads us to the third aspect of submission, the hands of submission. Because Paul loved all mankind, he chose to be a slave to all mankind. The choice to submit always leads to serving others. (More on service in the next lesson!)

In the famous *Carmen Christi* passage, Paul writes that Jesus "emptied Himself, taking the form of a bond-servant, and being made in the likeness of men" (Phil 2:7). Jesus didn't take the form of a man and become a like a servant; he took the form of a servant and was made in the likeness of men. The conscious decision of Jesus that led to his incarnation was to be a servant! Becoming a man was just the form he took to be able to serve.

Paul reiterates this point when he writes in Romans, "Let each of us please his neighbor for his good, to his edification. For even Christ did not please Himself..." (Rom 15:2-3). When we are living our lives to please others, we most resemble the life of Christ. But to please others, we must deny ourselves and be ready to render service to them.

Freedom!

Richard Foster has stated that there is a freedom corresponding to every discipline. I think he's right, but especially in regards to submission. He states, submission is freedom from "the terrible burden of always needing to have our own way" (Foster, 111). All these years you thought getting your way brought you freedom. In fact, it does not. Always having your own way means always having to be in control, always having to know everything going on around you, always having to be "in the middle of everything." You become entangled in every scheme, every plot, and every device of man. Having to have your own way is the greatest deception Satan ever accomplished on the people of God!

So what does the freedom of submission look like? It's the joy of gratitude from another. It's the love of mutual sacrifice. (Remember *The Gift of the Magi*?) It's the power of rendering service to others. It's the peace of an argument never had. It's the friendship never marred by a grudge. It's the marriage never ended by unfaithfulness. It's the church never split by opinions.

Submission defines and sets the parameters for how we will engage the world. If we cannot think of others as more valuable than ourselves, we will always engage the world for our own glory, and God's glory will never be present in our lives. If, however, we take every thought about every person around us "captive for the obedience of Christ," we will see them as Christ sees us all, love them as Christ loves us all, and serve them as Christ serves us all.

Seven Acts of Submissions

Foster's "Seven Acts of Submission" (Foster, 123-125) are listed below. They are more "authorities" to whom we submit, but the list works. I've rearranged them slightly to represent a "priority" in the event of conflicting interests. However, I believe if we understand the heart, head, and hands of submission, we will seldom experience any conflict. Instead, we will experience freedom from "existential angst" through the freedom of total self-denial.

To God: Thomas á Kempis summed it up best when he said, "As thou wilt; what thou wilt; when though wilt."[15] Without the attitude of total submission to God in every aspect of our life in every minute of our live, this discipline means nothing.

To Scripture: Foster clarifies a very important point about submission to God: "As we submit to the Word of God living (Jesus), so we submit to the Word of God written

---

[15] Thomas á Kempis, *The Imitation of Christ* in *The Consolation of Philosophy* (New York: Random House, 1943), 172.

(Scripture)."[16] Trying to follow God without following his revealed Word is the downfall of many well-meaning people.

To Church: Just as Foster said about submission to the Word of God living and the Word of God written, so it's true of the Word of God manifest—the church. To review to seek the good of the Lord's body is to diminish the Lord as the head of the body.

To Family: It's here that we first learn to care for the interest of others. Like a sport, it's to this fundamental we must always be true.

To Neighbors: As the story of the Good Samaritan teaches, no one is beyond our compassion and our assistance. No matter what the "perceived" cost, the "required" action is service in love.

To Needy: James 1:27 leaves no doubt that the purest of religion is caring for the needy. Regardless of theology, and often in spite of it, loving service to the needy defines Christianity.

To World (incl. Governments): God doesn't need rebels; he needs peacemakers. To submit to the authorities placed over us with godly humility brings peace to the world and to our souls.

---

[16] Foster, *Celebration*, 122.

Personal Practices

1. Reflect on Philippians 2:1-4.

   a. What are the driving forces behind submission?

   b. In what areas does submission encourage unity?

2. How can you live out the "heart" described in Ephesians 5:21-6:4 in your relationship with others?

3. Throughout one day, before answering any requests, say to yourself, "Because this person making this request is more important to me than I am to myself, I will...." This approach doesn't mean you have to do everything you are asked to do, but it does mean you have to carefully *and consciously* consider how you will respond to everyone you encounter.

Journal Reflections

1. In what areas are you uncompromisingly selfish? We all have areas we refuse to give up control of. Meditate on the book of Philippians and consider what area in your life is unconditionally "mine." Begin brainstorming ways that will help you give up control.

2. In what areas of your life has your pride infected the way you deal with others? Has it caused disunity? Discord? Unfaithfulness? Take these areas to God in prayer, confessing your pride and asking him to help you value others more.

SERVICE

Freedom from "the world's games"
(promotion, status, prestige, etc.)

As was mentioned a number of times in the last lesson, submission and service go hand-in-hand. Unless we develop an attitude of total submission, which equates to treating everyone as more important than yourself, your greatest act of service will always be lip service. Don't get me wrong; there can still be some great acts of service in our life. There was that time you drove the youth group to Timbuktu. There was that other time when you chaperoned a 30-hour lock-in which included fasting the entire time. Then there was that time when you used a week of vacation to go feed the hungry in some inner city mission. All in all, most of us can look back on several major projects we have undertaken in our lives and "chalk one up" for service.

Unfortunately, while all of these are valuable (especially to your youth minister!), they are not what service as a spiritual discipline is talking about. The discipline of service in the context of our study must be something that can be routinely practiced, not biennial works of greatness. These acts must also be a result of honing our skills in assessing all things spiritually and taking every thought captive for the obedience of Christ. With this understanding, service moves from acts of greatness to acts of grossness. Small, mundane, seemingly meaningless acts challenge our commitment to service much more than the grandiose accomplishments most of us think about: helping a young mom with a screaming baby—and her other three, small children; helping an elderly couple with their trays at a cafeteria—even while your food sits on your table getting cold; or stopping to help a family change a tire—even in the rain, on Sunday morning before church, in your best suit.

I know these are extreme examples. After all, no one wears a suit on Sunday morning anymore! But how many times have opportunities for service passed us by? I don't intend to make you feel guilty for being inconsiderate. I do intend to make you aware of how out of practice we are in discerning the needs of people around us. We aren't as selfish as we are oblivious, right? But is that really any better?

Jesus teaches that the small acts of service count. In fact, throughout the Bible, most of what we are asked to do is fairly small. We make Jesus' command to "deny yourself, take up your cross, and follow me" about huge acts of self-sacrifice. However, when Jesus teaches about Judgment Day (Matthew 25:31-46), he looks for people who have given water to the thirsty or clothes to the needy or visited the sick or imprisoned. We want to think that, unless the needy are in Cambodia or the prisoners are in Siberia, such small acts are inconsequential. According to Jesus, the smallest acts of service have eternal consequences.

Even in his own life, Jesus demonstrated this principle. Jesus, on the night before his arrest and eventual crucifixion, washed the feet of his disciples! If it had been me, my mind would have been running through a to-do list the length of my arm. But Jesus' list was very short; be a servant to his disciples. Prior to his greatest act of service to all mankind, Jesus served just a few in a small way.

Most Christians wait for the big projects before they jump in and serve. I don't think it's so much for the accolades of men as it is to make us feel better about our Christian walk. One great act has to compensate for passing up the many smaller ones, right? But Jesus demonstrated that service must be in the smallest way to the smallest (least) person. In truth, unless we live in daily service in the small things (like Jesus did) we won't be ready to serve in the big ways (like Jesus did) either.

In this same teaching, we learn another important lesson—how to view others. We've said that we must view others as more important than ourselves. In this short teaching, Jesus teaches us to view others as if they are Jesus himself! Talk about raising the bar! I know a lot of people who I consider better than myself, but none of them rank the same honor as Jesus—at least in my mind. But in the mind of Christ, something we are supposed to have because the Spirit dwells within us, everyone is worthy of the same treatment that would be given to him! This attitude of submission to others just as Christ "emptied himself" (Phil 2:5) for our benefit is the foundation of all acts of service, including Paul's description of the relationship between husband and wife in Ephesians 5.

Serving Doesn't Make You a Servant.

We've come full circle to last week's lesson. Service begins with submission. I can go to the food bank and pass out food, but that doesn't make me a servant *per se*. A king can disguise himself and live in poverty for a few weeks, but he neither stops being a king nor does he stop being rich. If he gave up his throne, sold all he had and gave it to the poor, moved into the 'hood, and served others with whatever resources he could find, he still would not be a servant. "Why not?" you ask. Because, servants have masters. Masters tell servants what to do. Servants do it without choice or expectation of gratitude, compensation, or even compassion.

This difficult truth is at the heart of Jesus' teaching in Luke 17:6-10. The master of the house has complete authority, and his needs overshadow the needs of the servant in every circumstance. Even after a long day working in the field, the servant must still come in and prepare a meal for the master. The servant cannot expect a break or even a hint of compassion. His path is determined by his status as servant.

As Christians we accept whatever path God has prepared for us. We can choose to run away from that path and reject the lordship of Christ, but we can't do so and still be a servant. We serve unceasingly and unconditionally. But how can service be rendered in this way? How can we serve with complete disregard for our own well-being? We do so because the love of Christ compels us.

In Paul's letter to the Corinthian church, he basically says, "I know I sound crazy when I talk about serving with such abandon, but it just flows from the love of Christ that drives everything in my life" (2 Corinthians 5:13-14a, wildly paraphrased!). He gives the foundation of this crazy service as the sacrificial love Jesus demonstrated for everyone by dying for all the world. If Jesus serves the world through death, then shouldn't we be ready to serve sacrificially as well?

Stress of Living Life to the Fullest

If we were honest with ourselves, we'd admit that the insane pursuit of prosperity and prestige is killing us. Almost every decision we make revolves around getting ahead in some way. Do I ask the boss not to curse around me or will that get me crossways with her? Do I sign-up for the Sunday shift so that the boss will know how committed I am to the job? If I don't go out drinking with my co-workers or peers will they think I'm unfriendly, or worse, intolerant of their lifestyle? This world and the things within it control every decision we make.

For a true servant of God, these choices aren't even available. Servants don't choose how to please themselves; they only choose how to please their master. If I know that I must be available to serve at the master's whim, I can't entangle myself in all of these worldly pursuits. I have to make sure that I am free whenever the master calls!

Wait, did I say, "Free"?

Is it possible that developing an attitude of submission and a willingness and readiness to serve sets me free? Being in service to God means I cannot be in service to the world. The world can't boss me around because the world is not my boss; God is my boss. And God is a jealous boss. If you work for him, no one else better mess with you. They may try, but God will intervene, just as he did for Israel on so many occasions. God likes his "good and faithful servants."

Imagine a life where you don't worry about getting that next promotion, or getting accepted by the right people, or making more money. Imagine a life that is filled with smiles of grateful people, hugs of encouraged children, tears of joyful widows, and blessings of a benevolent God. Are the benefits of serving ourselves really all that better than serving God?

Once again we must consider our previous disciplines of preparation. The kind of service that takes every thought captive for the obedience of Christ can only exist when a Christian has learned to be fully reliant on God's provision, fully trusting in God's promises, and filled fully by God's presence and God's word. The disciplines of preparation do not help us serve better; they help us become better servants. And so we return to our improved understanding of spiritual disciplines. They are not for receiving. They are for becoming.

David Srygley

Personal Practices

1. What characteristics of Christ must we possess to be a servant?

2. Why doesn't serving others equate to being a servant?

3. Look for opportunities to serve someone in such a way that his or her best interest is promoted and yours is diminished. Look for someone to serve who usually flies under the radar. Don't wait for something big; dive in and serve at the first opportunity.

Journal Reflections

1. In what area(s) of your life have you become a servant to this world? Who or what in these areas control the way you live your life? How can you set yourself free from them?

2. The life of a servant is difficult. In fact, since the Bible uses the word "slave" so regularly, we need to be prepared to serve in some of the ugliest, dirtiest ways—without any recognition. Therefore, only when we experience the love of Christ in our own lives can we serve others. Is your relationship with God strong enough and deep enough to commit your life to slavery for the sake of others? If not, how can it be strengthened?

CONFESSION

*Free to love and express our needs
and struggles openly.*

In Foster's presentation the discipline of Confession begins "Corporate Disciplines," the third set of four disciplines. Corporate disciplines are those that strengthen a Christian's walk by breaking down barriers between Christians and helping them integrate their lives into one body.[17] Dallas Willard did not have a specific term for these types of disciplines; however, he emphasized the role of fellowship in many of the same disciplines Foster calls corporate.[18]

"Corporate" confession is not about our need for the forgiveness of sins. Our prayers of repentance and forgiveness go from us through Christ our mediator to God (1 Timothy 2:5). Making this confession before men is not necessary for forgiveness of sin.

"Corporate" confession, instead, addresses the damage caused by sin, especially to the body of Christ and interpersonal relationships. In the Sermon on the Mount, Jesus instructs his listeners on corporate confession. "If therefore you are presenting your offering at the altar, and there remember that

---

[17] Foster, 145.
[18] Dallas Willard, *The Spirit of the Disciplines* (San Francisco: Harper, 1988), 186-187.

your brother has something against you, leave your offering there before the altar, and go your way; first be reconciled to your brother, and then come and present your offering" (Matt 5:23-24). The language isn't clear exactly who wronged who, but the action created animosity between two brothers. Jesus tells us to go and address that wrong and be reconciled to the brother.

How do you think that conversation went? There are a few options, but let's go with the simplest. The Christian who remembers that her brother is holding something against her goes to him and says, "I know you are upset about what happened yesterday. I'm really sorry. I made a huge mistake. Will you forgive me?" They discuss the situation, put it behind them, hug and they both return to worshipping God with their whole hearts. Because remember, the one who was angry is also told, "Do not let the sun go down on your anger" (Eph 4:26). Both Christians, by being at odds with one another, have placed themselves at odds with God's will.

God desires to extend forgiveness to everyone. He expects Christians, those reborn in his image, to do the same. The Model Prayer in Matthew 6:14-15 clearly states, "For if you forgive men for their transgressions, your heavenly Father will also forgive you. But if you do not forgive men, then your Father will not forgive your transgressions." God places a tremendous importance on forgiveness. He will only forgive his children in as much as they readily extend forgiveness to others. And by others he doesn't just mean other Christians. He says "forgive men."

So while corporate confession is not about our personal forgiveness of sin, it is about personally forgiving others with whom we have a God-ordained relationship. So then, the discipline of confession is a discipline of reconciliation. And like service, confession and reconciliation must flow from an attitude of submission!

Wholeness

If submission is the belief that others and their needs are more important than yourself and your needs, how does that attitude come into play in corporate confession? The simple answer is wholeness. Christians who believe their relationships with others are more important than their own pride or their own reputation or their own feelings will readily deal with the sin that has damaged those relationships. The relationship among believers is especially important as it demonstrates the unity of the church. Paul tells the Ephesians, "[W]alk in a manner worthy of the calling ... with all humility and gentleness, with patience, showing forbearance to one another in love, being diligent to preserve the unity of the Spirit in the bond of peace..." (Eph 4:2-3).

By confessing our sins to one another we declare a mutual dependence on God that results in healing, or "wholeness," and great works through prayer. I think this is what James has in mind when he pens, "Therefore, confess your sins to one another, and pray for one another, so that you may be healed. The effective prayer of a righteous man can accomplish much" (James 5:16). The confession of sins, one to another, and the prayers of the saints together lead to healing, or wholeness.

The word translated "healed" can also be translated "made whole." Since the passage is talking about praying for the sick, "healed" appears, at first glance, to be the appropriate word for the context. However, in verse 15, James has already told the church and elders to pray in faith for the sick so that they can be healed. Why turn around and say the *exact* same thing again? If we view verse 16 as instructions to the church and leadership as to how Christians should prepare themselves for prayer, the repeated instructions make more sense.

James says to pray for the sick for their restoration. But he tells the church, first confess your sins to each other and pray for each other. In other words, make sure that you as a church are "whole" (or "fully healthy") before you pray for those who are physically sick. Why do we need to make sure that we are spiritually whole and healthy? "The effective prayer of a *righteous* man can accomplish much" (James 2:16, emphasis added). Confessing to and praying for one another makes the church healthy, whole, and effective in prayer and ministry.

But if we are more worried about our reputation or pride than we are the health of the church, an obvious sign of a lack of submission, then we will never confess our sins to one another. It was noted in one of my evangelism classes at Southern Seminary that revivals have historically begun with spontaneous, authentic, public confession of sin.[19] If we want revival in the church today, perhaps this one discipline can bring it about.

Imperfect People Permitted

One last benefit of corporate confession needs to be mentioned. The public confession of sin validates an oft-repeated, but seldom-seen attribute of the church; we are an assembly of sinners saved by grace. We are not perfect. While we strive for maturity in our walk with Christ, we stumble—frequently. Corporate, or public, confession turns that failure in our own life into an opportunity to grow the church by demonstrating three important characteristics.

First, confession says that we are humble. It's not us who has the power to be victorious over sin; it's God. Confession

---

[19] Timothy Beougher, "History of Evangelism" (class lecture), The Southern Baptist Theological Seminary, 2013.

acknowledges our humble need for that ongoing salvation through the blood of Christ. Second, confession says that we are authentic and honest. We all sin—and we all know it. Why do we hide it? The answer, of course, is pride. But we often say that we don't want to blemish the reputation of the church. Since corporate confession means "confession within the body" ("corpus" means body, right?), not every confession will be known by everyone. Also, those confessions that are made publicly do not blemish the church; they send a very clear message that our love for one another is authentic and unconditional—just like Christ's love for us. Finally, confession says that we desire restoration, both for ourselves and for the church. In other words, we put the need of the church above our own.

Practicing the New Paradigm

So how does the practice of corporate confession help us in our new paradigm for spiritual discipline? How can confession, or any other corporate discipline that revolves around the church, help us to take captive every thought for obedience to Christ? How can it help us evaluate everything spiritually? The answer is surprisingly simple.

The center of the discipline of confession is that the health of the church is more important than the individual. More specifically, healthy relationships within the church, or any group in which a Christian is involved, are more important than his or her own best interest. As we practice the discipline of confession within the church body, we become better at assessing the impact of our decisions on the body. We become better at acknowledging when we've acted selfishly. We become better at seeing how a decision might impact others and therefore can avoid making those decisions which hurt those relationships. In short, we become more loving in our relationship with others, particularly in group settings.

Confession also teaches us how to deal with situations that could potentially damage those relationships with others and groups. Again, what we do is surprisingly simple. We must learn to seek reconciliation and restoration. If there is animosity between two people, the Christian is to take the first step in repairing that damaged relationship. Christians should always be the first to say, "I'm sorry." We also need to demonstrate humility towards others. Simply saying, "Will you forgive me," demonstrates how much we value the other person or persons.

Finally, confession teaches us to forgive others. When James says to confess our sins to one another, he also says pray for one another. The reconciliation through prayer can only occur if we readily forgive those who have wronged us. And if we understand the truth of submission, and practice it with our whole hearts, we won't have to wait for the other person to ask for that forgiveness. We extend it to them because they need restoration as much as we do.

Personal Practices

1. How does "corporate confession" differ from confession for the forgiveness of sins? In what ways does it still lead to forgiveness and wholeness?

2. How have your actions in the past, both at church and in the world, compromised the integrity and wholeness of a group of people?

3. Confession is late in our study because it cannot be practiced without the foundations of the other disciplines. Begin praying for those you have offended or for those against whom you hold a grudge. You may have to withdraw for a time to really examine your life and heart, but you will be blessed. Once identified, seek them out and simply say, "I'm sorry." Let the Spirit guide the remainder of your conversation.

Journal Reflections

1. Use your journal to confess your own sins to God. Bear your soul to him and experience his peace. The joy that you experience from his forgiveness will empower your desire to make amends with others.

2. Reflect on relationships that you can strengthen. In what areas of your life—church, work, family, friends—do you need to demonstrate more humility and willingness to put the needs of the group above your own?

3. Is there someone in your life that you need to forgive—and apologize to for holding a grudge?

WORSHIP

Our response to the reality of God.

All that I have seen teaches me to trust the Creator for all that I have not seen.
—Ralph Waldo Emerson

I'm a bit of a geek, or nerd, or whatever the word today is. Most people think of geeks and nerds as those who love computers, play chess, read sci-fi and fantasy books, and have to make straight A's in school. But that's not what defines a true geek. Geeks love to discover! We love to dig deep, ask questions—especially those questions no one else has thought to ask, and uncover bits and pieces of knowledge that have eluded the rest of the world. Everyone knows that there are facts still to be discovered in this world; geeks can't rest until we discover some of them.

Why are geeks motivated by this search? Because reality is awesome! Look around you and you can't help but be amazed at God's creation. If what we can see is awesome, imagine how awesome what we can't see is! Along those lines, the Intelligent Design discussion looks at the awesomeness of creation and declares, "There must be a Designer/Creator!" The declaration that there is a God and that he is awesome is the starting point of the discipline of Worship.

My Part in Worship

Our worship of God doesn't depend on God; it depends on us. God is awesome, period. He is awesome regardless of what is going on in our lives, in our families, at our workplaces, and even at our churches. (Remember we discussed this in our study on Prayer!) Worship, then, is how well we respond to this reality in spite of and in the midst of our circumstances. And this is why it's a spiritual discipline.

As a spiritual discipline, worship involves a number of "steps." Like many physical exercise regimens, this discipline builds upon a series of smaller exercises. However, instead of working through muscle groups and cardio fitness levels, worship requires Christians to work through and build upon several spiritual truths that work together to facilitate true worship.

One God

Worship of God is exclusive. We cannot worship God and ...! The Ten Commandments begins with this simple truth, "You shall have no other gods before Me" (Exo 20:3). It's not necessary to enumerate all the possible gods that we can place alongside the one, true God. We all know that at times we have put God second in our lives—or third, fourth, fifth, etc. Jesus tells us that Christians cannot serve two masters, "for he will hate the one and love the other, or he will hold to one and despise the other" (Matt 6:24). To fully worship God we must be fully committed to him.

One Confession

The writer of Hebrews reminds us that "a sacrifice of praise to God" (Heb 13:5) only comes from lips that confess his name. The NASB translates "confess" as "give thanks," which is fine. However, even giving thanks to God requires that we first confess his name. Since Hebrews 13:15-19 addresses Christian actions in regard to others, I can't help but think that the confession to which he refers is public. Not in the sense of public confession of sin before the congregation, but the kind of public confession Jesus refers to in Luke 12:8, "And I say to you, everyone who confesses Me before men, the Son of Man shall confess him also before the angels of God..."

Perhaps it's a no-brainer, but worship of God can't happen if we pretend like we don't know him! Maybe that's why we want to confine worship to Sunday morning church; it's safe there among other pretenders. But Jesus challenges us to confess his name before all men everywhere. When we confess our love for and allegiance to God, our worship has already begun!

One Grace

Without an understanding of grace it's impossible to worship God. If we think that we deserve salvation or have earned or merited it in any way, our hearts will never cry out to the Lord with unlimited thanksgiving and joy. As Peter describes it,

> But you are A CHOSEN RACE, A royal PRIESTHOOD, A HOLY NATION, A PEOPLE FOR God's OWN POSSESSION, that you my proclaim the excellencies of Him

who has called you out of darkness into His
marvelous light; for you once were NOT A
PEOPLE, but now you are THE PEOPLE OF
GOD; you had NOT RECEIVED MERCY,
but now you have RECEIVED MERCY. (1
Pet 2:9-10)

We didn't deserve God's calling or his mercy, but because
he chose to show us mercy and grace, we become his people
so that we can tell everyone how great he and his grace are.

Paul describes the extreme nature of this change in our
lives in Ephesians 2:1-10. In particular, he writes, "But God,
being rich in mercy, because of His great love with which
He loved us, even when we were dead in our transgressions,
made us alive together with Christ (by grace you have been
saved)..." (Eph 2:4-5). Because of God's love, mercy, and
grace, he has taken us in our death and made us alive with
Christ! Or as he describes in Colossians, "For He delivered
us from the domain of darkness, and transferred us to the
kingdom of His beloved Son" (Col 1:13). Again, without
grasping the change wrought in our lives because of God's
grace, our praise will ring hollow in our minds and mouths
and in his ears.

One Spirit and Truth

The story of the Samaritan woman that Jesus met at the well
of Jacob (John 4:7-30) has always provided a solid foundation
for worship. Jesus states unequivocally, "the true worshipers
shall worship the Father in spirit and truth" (John 4:23).
How a Christian ought to worship should not be a point of
disagreement. However, the "where" of the "how" is often
overlooked.

The discussion between Jesus and the Samaritan woman begins with the question of where to worship. Should men worship in Jerusalem or on Mount Gerizim? In most case we jump immediately to the how. Worshipers of God should do so in spirit and truth. But we skip right over Jesus' answer to her question. He replies, "There is no where. There is only a how." Both of these answers are important to our understanding of worship. We must be able to worship in spirit and truth anywhere.

If that is true, and I believe it is, then Christians must live in spirit and truth in every situation. That may seem like a tall order, but it's the essence of Jesus' answer. Man won't worship through rituals performed on a mountain or in a temple; he'll worship in his heart everywhere he goes. In order to practice worship as a discipline we must live in spirit and truth in every situation. We can't set aside our Christianity in order to take care of some worldly business. If we are to worship daily, we must walk daily in spirit and truth.

One Lord

To become a Christian we must confess Jesus as Lord (Romans 10:9). This confession begins our relationship with Christ but should define it as well. We are servants to the Most High God. We should consider it a privilege to serve in his kingdom—regardless of what he asks of us. Every opportunity to serve is an opportunity to worship and praise God.

God is in control and is ever present in this world and in our lives. He is Creator, Sustainer, and King. The greatest leap of faith is acknowledging that whatever happens, God can use it for good. Worshipping God involves learning to expect grace and goodness from God even when situations would appear to dictate otherwise.

Proverbs 3:5-6 reminds us, "Trust in the LORD with all your heart, And do not lean on your own understanding. In all your ways acknowledge Him, And He will make your paths straight." Because God is in control we know that all things will work to his glory. As servants of God, we can rejoice only when we love our master and trust him completely—even when we don't understand what he is doing. Being a child of God is a lot like, well, being a child! We just have to trust that he loves us, has great plans for us, and will take care of us.

Why Corporate?

Worship is readily and most often recognized as a corporate act. We attend worship services, or "praise and worship" services—as if the two are separate activities. Some refer to the church building as a house of worship. And others talk about "going to worship" on Sundays. All of these references indicate a disturbing pattern of assigning worship to a place and a time when Christians gather. Certainly worship should occur in our assemblies, but not exclusively. In fact, if worship is not occurring in the individual lives of each Christian, there is little chance that the individual Christian will experience much in the way of worship when he assembles with the saints!

So why use corporate language at all? As was mentioned in the discipline of confession, "corporate" literally means body. However, instead of defining a discipline as corporate because it's something that we participate in together, corporate disciplines would be better defined as disciplines that strengthen or are strengthened by the body of Christ. In other words, confession is corporate because it strengthens and repairs the relationships between members of the body. We might even say that confession is holistic medicine for the spiritual body. Worship is corporate because it is strengthened by assembling together and it enhances the joy of our mutual salvation in Christ.

Conclusion

With these truths firmly in hand we have a firm foundation for worshipping God. We begin with acknowledgement and acceptance of who God is. We must then recognize and acknowledge God's great work in our lives, both in salvation and in our on-going walk with him. Finally, we allow the Spirit to work through us in every situation to render service to God and to others. Worship, as was defined earlier, is how well we respond to the reality of God in spite of and in the midst of our circumstances. Circumstances may change, but the truth of God doesn't.

Truth	Worship
One God	Full commitment to our Creator & Sustainer.
One Confession	Public acknowledgement of God in our lives.
One Grace	Recognition of God's gift of reconciliation and his ability to continually transform us.
One Spirit and Truth	Ability to worship anywhere.
One Lord	Joy of being called to serve the King.

The movement from initial commitment to God to public worship through his Spirit in every situation will not be without obstacles and setbacks. The world doesn't mind if we believe in God as long as we keep it to ourselves. But as we mature in our spirituality, and our faith continues to integrate into more and more parts of our lives, we won't be able to stave off the worship; it will come from our lips with every breath.

At this point we return to our recurring theme. The discipline of worship teaches Christians to worship God in every situation. To do so we must assess every situation spiritually, looking for the presence of God, trusting in his sovereignty, rejoicing that he works in mysterious ways. We then must take the thoughts of those situations captive for obedience to Christ. We are commanded to rejoice always (1 Thes 5:16). So let's do away with grumbling, complaining, back-biting, and derision and give praise and glory to the God who deserves our worship whether the situation appears to dictate so or not.

Personal Practices

1. How does each of the five "Ones" contribute to a growth in worship?

2. Our worship of God requires a heart of praise pouring forth from the Spirit of truth within us. Look for times throughout the day when the Word of God contacts "the world" and gives you hope, strength, guidance, etc. When you see God with you and guiding you by his word, praise him aloud!

Journal Reflections

1. How well do you know God? Our praise comes from a heart filled with Spirit and truth. Consider the last several weeks of this study. Are you growing in your knowledge and understanding of God?

2. The discipline of worship helps us acknowledge that God's presence and awesomeness transcend the situation in which we find ourselves. Does your worship of God transcend the situations in which you find yourself or is it tied to how you feel about that situation?

3. Since the discipline of worship begins with having only one god, consider what idols may be in your life that would prevent you from worshipping God. What is robbing God of the worship and praise due him?

GUIDANCE

The Highest Level of Fellowship

There must also come a knowledge of the direct,
active, immediate leading of the Spirit *together*.
—Richard Foster, *Celebration of Discipline*

You must be asking yourself by now, "Is the discipline of guidance going to be a corporate discipline also? And if so, what does that mean?" These are both good questions, and both will be answered. However, I believe that you probably already know the answers. If "corporate" basically revolves around valuing the body of Christ more than our own body, how would you think guidance would be corporate?

You may not want to answer that question. The answer is filled with implications that rugged, individualistic Christians won't like—at all! Setting the stage for the answer, by couching it in terms of value and submission, sends up red flags. Such a context sounds as if guidance as a corporate discipline involves Christians subjecting themselves to the will of the church for the benefit of the church. The reason it sounds that way is because it is that way!

Willard doesn't call this discipline "guidance;" he calls it "submission," writing, "The highest level of fellowship—involving humility, complete honesty, transparency, and at times confession and restitution—is sustained by the discipline of submission."[20] "The highest level of fellowship" precisely captures the nature of the discipline of guidance; I'll do what's best for the body—as defined by the body—no matter what it costs me.

The Church is One

In olden days a particularly horrendous form of torturous death was quartering. It's exactly as the name implies. A person's left hand was tied to one horse, his right hand to different horse, and so with his two feet and two more horses. The horses were then prodded to bolt—in four different directions. The result was quartering.

This punishment was remarkably painful because the parts of the human body were never intended to go in different directions! One body, many parts, same direction! Too often we forget that the same is true for the body of Christ: one body with many members (1 Cor 12:12). And like any body it needs to move in the same direction lest disaster follows.

Paul teaches the church to "preserve the unity of the Spirit in the bond of peace. *There is* one body and one Spirit, just as you were called in one hope of your calling; one Lord, one faith, one baptism, one God and Father of all who is over all and through all and in all" (Eph 4:3-6). Though the New American Standard Bible, the New International Version, and other translations start a new sentence in verse 4, the verse begins with a relative pronoun in the Greek, which. The "is" is understood from the grammar. So actually the verse states that "the unity of the Spirit in the bond of peace" *is*

---

[20] Willard, *The Spirit of the Disciplines*, 189.

"one body..." The unity and peace experienced by the church is fully dependent upon the reality that the church is one.

As a result of focusing on the one mission of the church and on the truth on which it is to be built, the church grows into Christ "from whom the whole body, being fitted and held together by that which every joint supplies, according to the proper working of the individual part, causes the growth of the body for the building up of itself in love" (Eph 4:16). Paul makes three important points in this passage.

First, the goal is "to grow up in all aspects into Him, who is the head, even Christ" (Eph 4:15). This goal accords with the goal of the Christian to mature into Christ's likeness and, as we've been discussing, to grow in all aspects. But the growth mentioned here is not just individual growth, it's the growth of the body "for the building up itself in love." Christians grow so that the church can grow.

Second, the church is held together by the individuals. Sometimes we don't think we play an important part in the church's mission, but consider what Paul writes. "[B]eing fitted and held together by that which every joint supplies, according to the proper working of the individual part" (Eph 4:16). The body is held together by that which every joint supplies. The bond that holds the church together is supplied by the parts of the body! That means the body's unity is up to each of us.

Finally, Paul says that the parts supply the bond when they are working properly. Each part has a purpose and a calling. When we do well what God has called us to do, we contribute to the unity and growth of the church. When we shirk our responsibilities or give it less than our best effort, the unity and growth of the church suffer!

The prophet Malachi had to repeatedly chastise Israel for short-changing God. Their sacrifices were pathetic, their teachings were lies, and their tithes were tokens. While they went through the motions, their heart was far from God. As a result, God withdrew from Israel, and we don't hear from him again until he arrives among us as the incarnate Christ. (Malachi is the last prophet before the four hundred years of silence we call the "intertestamental period." After those four hundred years Christ comes to preach the gospel of God to all people.)

The discipline of guidance as a corporate discipline begins with the recognition that each of us is an integral part of God's plan for the church. It also requires us to value God's plan for the church above any plans we may make for ourselves. In other words, we must have a submissive attitude towards the church.

All for One, and One for All

In Acts 15 we have the record of the council at Jerusalem. The story involves a discussion of what the church should teach about circumcision and the keeping of the law. After hearing the accounts of the work of God among the Gentiles, James makes the decision that Gentiles be held to basic principles of the law and not the specifics (Acts 15:20). Though James makes the proclamation, it's important to look at all that is going on.

First, a "multitude" is involved in hearing the stories of Barnabas and Paul (Acts 15:12). Second, when the decision is made, the apostles, the elders, and "the whole church" decided it was good to select men to take the message to everyone (Acts 15:22). And finally, James declares, "For it seemed good to the Holy Spirit and to us…" (Acts 15:28). The decision proclaimed was in accordance with the will of God and the will of the people in submission to him. The church, her leaders, and the Spirit are to be unified in purpose and action.

Another example of unified purpose and action is the process given by Jesus in Matthew 18:15-20 for church discipline. Church discipline became very unpopular for many decades, but it has seen growing support among Christian leaders. Jay Adams, in *Handbook of Church Discipline* (1986), Donald Whitney, in *Spiritual Disciplines Within the Church* (1996), and Mark Dever, in *Nine Marks of a Healthy Church* (2004), address the need for the church to discipline her members. Of course, in order for a church to discipline her members, the members must have a spirit of submission!

Jesus' statement about the power of unified action should not be overlooked or downplayed. The discipline process begins at an individual level, between two brothers in Christ, but then moves to a larger circle by including other "witnesses" (Matt 18:16). "Witnesses" implies that the need to provide guidance to a Christian has already moved from individual to corporate. In the final phase of discipline, the entire church becomes involved. If the individual Christian will still not submit to the guidance of the entire congregation, then the congregation is to put him out of the church.

The church having the power to decide someone's spiritual health scares many Christians. "Who are you to pass judgment on my 'spirituality'?" is the common response. But Jesus, as if anticipating this situation, states,

> Truly I say to you, whatever you shall bind on earth shall be bound in heaven; and whatever you loose on earth shall be loosed in heaven. Again I say to you, that if two of you agree on earth about anything that they may ask, it shall be done for them by My Father who is in heaven. For where two or three have gathered together in My name, there I am in their midst. (Matt 18:19-20)

The church, when gathered in the name of Jesus, assumedly to do his will, has the authority of God to act. But Jesus being in the midst of the church should also give the church the wisdom needed to discern the truth. I think Jesus is saying, "Hey, I'm here to help!" What if we saw the church as God's means for strengthening our lives and giving our lives purpose? Would we come to church more eager to learn and with a greater spirit of humility and submission?

Shepherds as Guides

It's fairly easy to conceptualize elders and shepherds as spiritual leaders and decision-makers for the church. How a church spends her money, what doctrines are taught in the classes, and other corporate decisions should be the responsibility of elders. In fact, Paul affirms this understanding in Acts 20:28 when he tells the elders at Ephesus, "Be on guard for yourselves and for all the flock, among which the Holy Spirit has made you overseers, to shepherd the church of God which He purchased with His own blood." Elders shepherd the church. Got it!

But as we've learned, the lives of individual Christians must be integrated into the life and fiber of the church. For the integration of many members into one body, purpose, and action, those who make the decisions that guide the church must also be allowed to guide the individual members of it. Elders must be able to say, "Because the church needs *x*, we need you to do *y*."

Paul clearly expects elders and deacons to be good managers of individuals. When he instructs Timothy on the character and qualities of elders and deacons, Paul says to find men who can manage their children "with all dignity" (1 Tim 3:4). The other character traits listed in both First Timothy and Titus describe someone whose way of dealing with others brings glory and honor to God. Peter also instructs leaders to lead without "lording it over those allotted to your charge" (1 Peter 5:3).

Rubber Meets the Road

Does faith in God mean faith in his church? Does submitting to God's will mean submitting to his church? When we ask if our life glorifies God should we also ask if our life glorifies his church? When deciding what is best for me, do I consider what is best for the church? These last few questions dramatically change the focus of our decision-making and the need for guidance from the church.

When we make decisions, we usually inform the church about them. Seldom do we ask the church to be involved in them. We might ask for prayers that we can make the right choice, but again, seldom do we ask the leaders what is the right choice. Guidance as a discipline calls on us to start giving the church more say in our lives. If we are to have all things in common as the first century church did then we are going to have to start putting our whole life out on the table for everyone to see, to comment on, to direct, and to pray about.

It also calls for giving the needs and good of the church more weight in our decisions. When we weigh whether to take a new job in another city, we should consider how that move will impact the church. Since the church is one body in multiple locations, this impact can have two sets of possibilities. How will your current church respond to your departure? Are there people ready to take up the ministries with which you are involved? Have you made commitments that need to be met? On the other hand, what opportunities does God have in store for you at the church in your new community? How will you contribute there? Will you be able to continue serving effectively?

These questions that we need to consider make a pretty big assumption. They assume you care more about the good of the church than your own. So like so many other of our disciplines of engagement, we find ourselves back at submission—seeing the needs of others as greater than your own.

Personal Practices

1. How is the individual growth of a Christian related to the growth of the church?

2. Describe how submission is the foundation for guidance as a corporate discipline.

3. Schedule a meeting with an elder to discuss how you might contribute more to the church's growth. Ask them to honestly assess how they see you and your walk with God and your place in the church.

Journal Reflections

1. Are you the weakest link? An old game show used to ask that question in a quasi-team competition. Christians should be asking themselves the same question. Am I the weakest link? Am I holding the church back or helping it to grow stronger? In what areas might you be the weakest link?

2. Pursuing the will of God for your own life means you must consider how your life is intimately plugged into the life of the church. What areas of your life need to be redirected so that your life contributes to God's plan for his church?

CELEBRATION

"The joy of the Lord is my strength" (Neh 8:10)

We worship God for who He is; we celebrate for what He has done. We can only celebrate, then, when we know what God has done and is doing for us. For this reason, Bible study is critical; knowledge produces celebration. When we learned about Jesus' sacrifice on our behalf, we celebrated, right? But knowledge of what he has done to save us is only the foundation. We must discover each day what God continues to do for us and in us. Often we fail to recognize that God is continuously working in our lives. To truly celebrate God we must become aware of his hand in our lives every day. The more we find God working in us, the more we celebrate. Willard writes, "We engage in celebration when we enjoy ourselves, our life, our world, *in conjunction with* our faith and confidence in God's greatness, beauty, and goodness. We concentrate on *our* life and world as God's work and as God's gift to us."[21]

Perhaps celebration is the most difficult discipline because life isn't perfect. We lose sight of his "gracious provision" each day. Perhaps it's the discipline of disciplines. It's the culmination of all other disciplines as we bring our lives into submission to God and full integration of our faith and our world! Foster

---

[21] Willard, *Spirit*, 179.

places celebration last in his study for this reason. He writes, "Joy is the end result of the Spiritual Disciplines' functioning in our lives. God brings about the transformation of our lives through the Disciplines, and we will not know genuine joy until there is a transforming work within us."[22] Abiding joy in Christ is the product of a life transformed into Christ's likeness.

God is Good

Many a child has begun her thanksgiving prayer, "God is great. God is good. Let us thank him for our food." That prayer shouldn't have to change much as we get older. We realize that God is always great and he is always good. We also realize that "food" and "good" don't really rhyme, so we can substitute anything into this last part of this prayer! "God is great. God is good. Let us thank him for our health." In my mind, that works just fine! The beginning of celebration is recognition that God provides ... period.

Salvation is Good

When the angel to the shepherds, they announced, "I bring you good news of a great joy which shall be for all the people; for today in the city of David there has been born for you a Savior, who is Christ the Lord" (Luke 2:10-11). This passage says so much about our God. The good news was brought to us. The great joy was for all the people. The Savior was born for us. Every part of God's plan for our salvation was for us. It wasn't good news, great joy, or salvation for God or Jesus that Jesus had to leave heaven and the presence of his father, be tormented and ridiculed, and be put to death. It was all for us, and it was all good.

---

[22] Foster, *Celebration*, 193.

Provision is Good

God didn't provide just salvation, though even that was pretty great by itself. He also provides us with the blessings of life. Numerous times throughout the Sermon on the Mount, God's provision is emphasized. In the Lord's Prayer, he instructs us to pray for "daily bread" (Matt 6:11). In Matthew 6:25-34 Jesus reassures us that God loves us so much that he will always take care of us. He doesn't let the birds starve or the lilies of the field go naked; neither will he let us. And in Matthew 7:11 Jesus explains why God is so good to us. It's because he is so good.

Everything is Good

In the Sermon on the Mount, we are also reminded that the blessings of God flow to those who "seek first His kingdom and His righteousness" (Matt 6:33). While it's easy to ask God for blessings, it's much more difficult to ask for the blessings that flow from his kingdom. Most often we want the blessings that are available from this world. They are more tangible, more accessible, easier to flaunt, and easier to enjoy with little apparent cost. The blessings that flow from the kingdom of God are deeper and aren't as easily seen by others—and it seems like they always come at a greater cost. All three of these downsides of the blessings of God are true, that's why the upside of the blessings of God has to be worth the risk—and they are!

One of my favorite words in the New Testament, besides propitiation, is "all." Have you ever noticed how often it's used? I can't go through *all* the occurrences, but it's everywhere. One of the best Scripture with the word "all" is Romans 8:28, "And we know that God causes all things to work together for good to those who love God, and to those who are called according to His purpose." Rightfully so, there is some debate about the exact order of the words in the verse. Some translations, like the NASB above, the Holman Christian Standard Bible, the New International Version, and the King James Version, imply that the beneficiary of the good that is accomplished by God is the Christian. Other translations, like the Revised Standard Version and English Standard Version, imply that the good has a broader focus. "And we know that for those who love God all things work together for good, for those who are called according to his purpose" (Rom 8:28, ESV). In this translation, those who love God can be assured that everything will work out for good, whether that good is for the individual Christian, the church, or God's universal plan and will.

I prefer the latter translation. Christians experience events in life that are not good for them. Some of them are by circumstances beyond their control. Some, if not most, are by their own devices. Paul assures Christians that everything will be just fine if you trust God. Good for you? Maybe; maybe not. Good for God? Yes, indeed.

The story of Samson and Delilah in Judges 16 is a great example of this principle. Samson betrayed himself to Delilah by sharing the secret of his strength. He was captured and tortured—we'll skip the details. Ultimately, he was led into the arena to be scoffed at and likely abused for the entertainment of the Philistines. It was in that arena that Samson died when the building collapsed.

Now on the surface, there is nothing that can be identified as "all things work together for good to those who love the Lord." Samson loved God, but after imprisonment, torture, and ridicule, he died. So much for Samson's good. But the surface, as it often does in this world, distorts the truth below. In Samson's death was his greatest victory for God. Yes, he had gotten himself in quiet a pickle because of his pride. But after repenting, God gave him another chance to accomplish something great.

Samson died when the building collapsed because Samson destroyed the building's two middle pillars that held up the building. Did he know that he'd die if he did so? I'm pretty sure he knew how his actions were going to play out, but he did it for the good of God's people. (Notice how we keep coming back to submission and the role of the corporate mindset! I told you that you couldn't practice any of the disciplines of engagement without these two elements.) In fact, the Bible states, "So the dead whom he killed at his death were more than those whom he killed in his life" (Judges 16:30). All things did work together for good—if you are one who loves the Lord more than anything else!

If we want to see the goodness of God, we have to love him and follow his calling. As we discussed in the last lesson, we cannot forget that each of us plays an important and specific part in God's plan. When we lay everything else aside and serve him in his kingdom, all the goodness of the kingdom becomes ours as well. Celebration arises out of the joy that the goodness of the kingdom brings. And the goodness of God is both without measure and without conditions. God is always good in every situation, so the blessings we experience as servants in his kingdom are always good in every situation.

Submission, Obedience, and Celebration

Samson's story and Romans 8:28 both remind us of one other very important point. You have to be willing to do things God's way. Paul says everything works for good for those who love God and "are called according to His purpose" (Rom 8:28). Samson's purpose was to serve as a judge for

Israel and protect her from the Philistines. When his purpose was derailed by his arrogance, the situation turned bad fast. But once he was humbled before God, he recommitted to his purpose—to bring down the Philistines. And so he did, literally, by killing more in his death than in his life.

Obeying God may seem like an unfair condition for receiving God's blessings, but Jesus says as much. He taught his disciples, "If you keep My commandments, you will abide in My love; just as I have kept My Father's commandments, and abide in His love. These things I have spoken to you, that My joy may be in you, and that your joy may be made full" (John 15:10-11). God loves us and desires to bless us, but we must enter into and abide in that love. Jesus said the way to abide in that love is to keep his commandments.

Keeping his commandments also brings us his joy and makes our joy full, or complete. Jesus said, "[T]hese things I have spoken to you ..." Everything Jesus has taught us is so that we can have his joy. There may be other forms of joy in this world, but none of them amount to anything when compared to the joy of the Lord. Nehemiah understood this when he said, "The joy of the Lord is my strength" (Neh 8:10). The joy that comes from abiding in and obeying Christ's teachings makes you more than happy; it makes you powerful and it makes you blessed by God (Luke 11:28)!

The Discipline of Celebration

The practice of the discipline of celebration is four-fold. First, you must recognize the need to abide in and obey the word of God. This discipline looks back to and builds upon the disciplines of preparation discussed earlier. A thorough understanding of God through his word helps you discern what you should be doing in every situation. Obedience to the will of God is much easier when you know what the will of God looks like.

Second, you must believe that because you are living according to God's will for your life, God is actively involved with your life. The writer of Hebrews states, "And without faith it's impossible to please Him, for he who comes to God must believe that He is, and that He is a rewarder of those who seek Him" (Heb 11:6). Christians who seek God will receive something from God. That something, minimally, is God's provision and blessings. In other words, because you have sought after God, he will provide for you. The more difficult the situation is in which you find yourself, the greater the faith, the greater the seeking, and the greater the blessings.

Third, you must begin to see God working in your life. Believing that God is working in your life will produce a minimal level of celebration. Seeing God work in your life can produce unimaginable praise and celebration. It's nice to know your spouse loves you. It's even better when they rub your shoulders, bake you cookies, or go on long walks on the beach with you. If we really want to get better at celebrating God, we need to get better at seeing his hand in our lives.

Fourth, you must thank him for his provision in your life. We haven't spent much time on this part, but it stems from a basic premise. You won't celebrate the giver if you don't appreciate the gift. Paul warns that failing to give thanks can undermine even the best knowledge of God. He writes, "For even though they knew God, they did not honor Him as God, or give thanks; but they became futile in their speculations, and their foolish heart was darkened" (Rom 1:21). Between the best knowledge of God and the best celebration of God there is gratitude for God.

When you start walking through life looking at every event as an opportunity to praise God, you will get better and better at celebration. Little events become one more part of an incredible life God is working out for you.

Best of all, when we really begin practicing celebration, we'll get good at it. When circumstances appear to be stressful or depressing or hopeless, you can see God's hand. Others around you can't understand why you are content and feeling blessed in the middle of heartache, because they can't see what you see. When they see the devil's work, all they see is the devil. When Christians who have mastered the discipline of celebration see the devil's work, we see God's hand and God's victory.

Where Better Than the World

We need to be reassured of God's presence and provision in our lives. We need the joy of knowing that God is with us and that he is our strength. And we need that joy and strength, not in a pew on Sunday morning, but in every situation in every day of our lives. The discipline of celebration provides that reassurance, joy, and strength.

Remember, celebration is a result of recognizing what God has done. The practice of the discipline enhances our ability to see what God is doing and trust that it's good. As we go through each day, we are distracted by so many happenings and things. We are overwhelmed by this world; so much so that we can't see God around us. Because we don't experience God's presence, we don't draw on his strength and enjoy the Christian life he intends for us.

Equally true, we are overwhelmed by the negative. It only takes a few minutes of reading the morning newspaper or surfing the web to become discouraged by what is happening in the world. For many, it only takes a few minutes of interacting with coworkers or peers at school or family to become depressed or anxious. This world, regardless of and in spite of what it promises, cannot offer the strength, joy, and peace that God can provide. James' observation about the tongue is equally true of the world; "Can both fresh water and salt water flow from the same spring?" (James 3:11 NIV).

Considering the virtual impossibility of finding anything of substance and value in this world, is it any wonder that Jesus tells us to look elsewhere? "But seek first His kingdom and His righteousness, and all these things will be added to you" (Matt 6:33). Though Jesus is specifically referring to food and clothing, the implication goes way beyond those essentials. The Sermon on the Mount and, especially, the Beatitudes offer rest, mercy, satisfaction, and more. Who wouldn't want to celebrate a God who makes—and faithfully keeps—promises like these?

Corporate, Too?

Finally, we arrive at the question we've asked several times. How is this discipline corporate? We've been working with the definition of corporate discipline that emphasizes relationship with others, and particularly the body of Christ. We've learned that submission is critical to the practice of corporate disciplines. We must perceive the needs of others and of groups of which we are a part as more important than our own individual needs. As a result of prioritizing the relationship with others, corporate disciplines are those disciplines that help strengthen those relationships or help strengthen us by practicing them in relationship with others. Celebration does both.

The latter is much easier to experience. We go to church and are uplifted by the songs of praise, the testimonies of people with answered prayers, and the camaraderie of saints sharing stories of victory over Satan and sin. Maybe because I am the preacher people like to talk to me about what is happening in their lives, and I'm glad they do. I'm encouraged and my joy is made complete when I hear how God is working in the lives of the people I love. In an odd way, it's Nehemiah 8:10 in disguise; the joy of the saints is my strength!

But assembling with the saints also strengthens the saints. Growing up in a Christian home we are taught by our parents, or at least I was taught by mine, that you don't always go to church for yourself. You go for God and for others. I hear my parents' words to me and my wife's words to our kids, "You being at church may be the encouragement that someone else needs." Who knew then that our parents were trying to help us grasp and practice the corporate spiritual discipline of celebration!

I think it's important to remember that our circumstances don't determine which of these two benefits will be derived from going to church. You may be going through a very difficult time in your life and go to church to help you find peace in God's presence. In sharing your struggles, you receive the encouragement and prayers of others, but you might turn out to be the encouragement someone else needed at the same time. We've all heard stories of people sharing their struggles with a group only to have someone else in the group say, publicly or privately, "I'm really sorry about your problems, but I'm going through something similar and it was good to know I'm not alone."

Personal Practices

1. In what ways has God provided "good" to all the world?

2. How does obedience to God produce "abiding joy"?

3. Consider the things that make you happy and weigh whether they produce the deep abiding joy of the Lord or just a hollow emotional high. The next time you have an opportunity to make a choice, weigh the decision by asking which choice will bring the sustaining "joy of the Lord" and which will only bring temporary pleasure.

Journal Reflections

1. Jesus asks the question, "For what does it profit a man to gain the world, and forfeit his soul?" (Mark 8:36). In what areas of your life currently do you not feel God is adequately providing and that you need more than what He is willing to give?

2. Consider how God has taken care of other areas of your life in the past and celebrate his provision. Does doing so build confidence in trusting God?

APPENDIX ONE

Biblical and Theological Support for the
Role of Spiritual Growth in Evangelism

God made two important decisions in his plan for the growth of the kingdom. First, he decided one must hear the good news of Christ's salvific work prior to being saved. Second and closely related to the first, he decided to use disciples as his instruments, or mouthpieces, for proclaiming the good news of Jesus' death, burial, and resurrection. In this chapter, we'll consider the Scriptural support for both of these premises in the first part of this chapter. After such consideration, we will then discuss the Scriptural support for the role of spiritual growth in Christians in the proclamation of the gospel.

The Necessity of Hearing

In Romans 10:9-17 the apostle Paul asserts that an authoritative word must be heard and understood before one can be saved. This word can only be heard if messengers of God authoritatively proclaim it.[23] John Stott supports this point in his excellent and oft repeated sequence of salvation: "Christ sends heralds; heralds

---

[23] Joseph Fitzmeyer, *Romans*, Anchor Bible (New York: Doubleday, 1993), 596. While Fitzmeyer has the bishopric in mind when he speaks of "someone who is authorized," the same authorization exists for all in the priesthood of the believers (1 Pet 2:9).

preach; people hear; hearers believe; blievers call; and those who call are saved."[24] Thomas Schreiner affirms this sequence, "The steps of the chain must be realized if people are going to call on the Lord and be saved."[25] Douglass Moo concurs when he writes, "Paul creates a connected chain of steps that must be followed if a person is to be saved (v. 13)."[26] These scholars agree that there is a definite *ordo salutis*, placing hearing the gospel before believing it.

More precisely, Schreiner places significant emphasis on the necessity of hearing the gospel message. Though natural revelation provides a foundation for an understanding of the existence of God, it's insufficient; this insufficiency is evidenced by the idolatry that often results from focusing exclusively on nature.[27] Schreiner notes, "Romans 10:14-17 ... excludes the idea that salvation can be obtained apart from an external hearing of the gospel."[28] Though this statement appears to underestimate the power of God's Word to work effectually through reading, Schreiner's point is still valid: people cannot discover God's plan for salvation unless another exposes them to it. Moo states, "Hearing, the kind of hearing that can lead to faith, can only happen if there is a definitive salvific word from God that is proclaimed."[29] Moo, Schreiner, and Joseph Fitzmeyer concur that the use of Isaiah in the course of Paul's argument in Romans 10 affirms that "hearing" has always

---

[24] John Stott, *The Message of Romans* (Downers Grove, IL: Inter-Varsity Press, 1994), 286.

[25] Thomas Schreiner, *Romans,* Baker Exegetical Commentary on the New Testament (Grand Rapids: Baker, 1998), 567.

[26] Douglas Moo, *The Epistle to the Romans*, New International Commentary on the New Testament, rev. ed. (Grand Rapids: Eerdmans, 1968), 663.

[27] Schreiner, *Romans*, 568.

[28] Ibid.

[29] Moo, *Romans*, 666.

been a part of God's plan for the proclamation of his will for his people, including his plan for saving them.[30]

The Necessity of Proclaiming

Since non-Christians must hear the gospel, it becomes incumbent upon Christians to proclaim it. In his Great Commission, Christ charges all Christians to "make disciples" (Matt 28:19-20). While some might argue that this commission only applied to the original disciples, D. A. Carson rightly concludes that the commission "is binding on all Jesus' disciples to make others what they themselves are—disciples of Jesus Christ."[31] In this text the manner by which discipleship is accomplished is teaching. Carson states, "Matthew's gospel ends with the expectation of continued mission and teaching."[32] Carson further points out that the preceding five narrative sections in Matthew (3:1-26:5) end with blocks of teaching by Jesus, "but the passion and resurrection of Jesus end with a commission to his disciples to carry on the same ministry" of teaching.[33]

R. T. France draws a similar conclusion when he notes that, in the Great Commission, "Jesus transfers the duty of teaching from himself to the disciples."[34] Along with that duty came the authority of Jesus and the content of what was

---

[30] Moo, *The Epistle to the Romans*, 666; Schreiner, *Romans*, 569; and Fitzmeyer, *Romans*, 596.

[31] D. A. Carson, *Matthew* in vol. 8 of *The Expositor's Bible Commentary*, ed. Frank E. Gaebelein (Grand Rapids: Zondervan, 1995), 596.

[32] Ibid., 599.

[33] Ibid.

[34] R. T. France, *The Gospel of Matthew*, The New International Commentary on the New Testament, rev. ed. (Grand Rapids: Eerdmans, 2007), 1118.

to be taught Jesus himself.[35] Donald Hagner concurs, "It's the particular responsibility of the church to hand on that teaching and see to it that new disciples make it their way of life."[36] Jesus' authority (28:18) and his presence (28:20b) empower and ensure the church in her call and commission to teach.[37]

Ulrich Luz concludes that Matthew viewed the church as "basically and fundamentally a missionary church."[38] Particularly insightful is Luz' observation that, in Matthew, "there is no Paraclete who replaces Jesus and 'leads (the disciples) into all the truth' (John 16:13); instead, Matthew binds the proclamation of the church permanently and solely to the proclamation of Jesus."[39] If the church does not proclaim "all" that Christ has commanded, and teach Christ's followers to "obey" those things, the church has no other hope. Luz' observation is not meant to belittle the role of the Holy Spirit, but to challenge Christians to accept the critical importance of evangelism in God's plan.

Luz, however, places "teaching them to obey all that I have commanded you" at the center of the Great Commission. Though Luz appears to downplay the role of baptism and conversion in the Great Commission,[40] his important conclusion is that "according to Matthew the only witness to the risen Jesus is one's own praxis of discipleship in the community of disciples, the church."[41] If the church does

---

[35] Ibid.

[36] Donald Hagner, *Matthew 14-28*, Word Biblical Commentary Series (Dallas: Word Books, 1995), 888.

[37] Ibid., 889.

[38] Ulrich Luz, *Matthew 21-28*, Hermeneia (Philadelphia: Fortress Press, 2005), 628.

[39] Ibid., 633.

[40] Ibid., 634.

[41] Ibid,, 636.

not teach disciples to teach new disciples to live according to the teachings of Christ, no valid witness to the truth of the resurrection of Christ will exist. In short, Christians' behaviors can undermine the message of the Great Commission.

Moo, in his comments on Romans 10:9-14, supports this conclusion when he observes that Paul uses "disobedience" in place of "disbelief." Moo points out that Paul pairs disobedience with Isaiah's "believe" in Isaiah 53:1; a substitution that continues Paul's connection of faith and obedience begun in Romans 1:5 with "obedience of faith."[42] One could argue that Jesus makes the same relationship between obedience and evangelism in the Great Commission when he says "teaching them to *observe* all that I commanded you" (Matt 28:19, emphasis added).

Though only two passages have been considered, the relationship between the necessity of hearing and the necessity of proclamation is clear. Salvation comes to all those who hear and call upon the name of the Lord, but hearing presupposes proclamation. Paul's use of Isaiah's rhetorical question, "Have they not heard?" affirms that Paul believed that people would hear—and then would have a choice. This expectation would only seem valid if Paul had believed that the word was being proclaimed throughout the world. Since that is the case then the only people Paul could have expected to proclaim that message are Christians themselves.

But these two passages also introduce Christians to the idea that a relationship exists between evangelism and an obedient lifestyle. The commentators cited above agree that the Great Commission places discipleship at the center of the church's mission. But the church must meet two conditions if it's to be a "missionary church." First, Christians must proclaim the gospel. Secondly, Christians must live an

---

[42] Moo, *The Epistle to the Romans*, 665.

obedient life to the teachings of Christ to affirm or give witness to the truth of the gospel.

Christians should not underestimate the importance of living and proclaiming the gospel. Salvation comes only to those who "call upon the name of the Lord," and they can only call if they have heard the truth of the death, burial, and resurrection of Jesus Christ (Rom 10:9-10). Christians need to accept that they are responsible for the proclamation of the gospel and the salvation of those people with whom God has brought them into contact. Taking this responsibility seriously, Christians will grow in their own walk with God so their lives and their words can be valid testimonies to the saving work of Christ.

The Necessity of Spiritual Growth in Evangelism

If both what Christians know and share and how they live their lives are foundational for evangelism, then spiritual growth becomes essential to the fulfillment of the Great Commission. Paul makes this connection between the growth of the gospel in the world and the spiritual growth of the individual clear in Colossians 1:6-12.

In Paul's estimation, the growth of the gospel in the world corresponds to growth in individual Christians. Thus Moo writes, "In v. 6, the focus was on the extension of the gospel to many people; here, however, it's the intensive growth within each believer that is the focus."[43] N. T. Wright provides a similar insight: "Just as the gospel is bearing fruit and growing, so God's people are themselves *bearing fruit in every good work*, and *growing in the knowledge*

---

[43] Douglas Moo, *The Letter to the Colossians and to Philemon*, Pillar New Testament Commentary (Grand Rapids: Eerdmans, 2008), 97.

of God."[44] Wright rightly posits that the addition of "in every good work" to "bearing fruit" and "in the knowledge of God" to "growing" expands the "formula of v. 6" to include both the active and reflective aspect of Christianity.[45] Stated differently, the growth in *and* the fruit of the gospel in the world produces, and is produced by, good works and knowledge of God in and through Christians themselves.

The gospel growing throughout the world while Christians themselves are dying apart from the vine is hard to envision. F. F. Bruce makes this connection when he writes, "The fair fruit of good works would spring in greater abundance from the divine seed which has been sown in their hearts, *and at the same time* they would make ever increasing progress in the knowledge of God."[46] Growing Christians produce greater fruit when they are actively engaged in good works.

The growth of the individual that results in the growth of the gospel is not simply an increase in knowledge. According to Wright, "this knowledge is given *through all spiritual wisdom and understanding.* Knowledge of God's will *manifests itself in* these qualities."[47] The knowledge cannot stand alone as the source of growth; it must be accompanied by or produce in Christians wisdom and understanding. But this wisdom and understanding, described as spiritual, is only visible to the world through "good works." Wright states,

> For Christians to "grow up" in every way will include the awakening of intellectual powers,

[44] N. T. Wright, *Colossians and Philemon*, Tyndale New Testament Commentaries (Downers Grove, IL: IVP Academic, 2008), 59.

[45] Ibid.

[46] F. F. Bruce, *Commentary on the Epistle to the Colossians* in The New International Commentary on the New Testament, 1st ed. (Grand Rapids: Eerdmans, 1977), 186.

[47] Wright, *Colossians and Philemon*, 58; emphasis original.

the ability to think coherently and practically about God and his purposes for his people. The wisdom and understanding commended here are given the adjective 'spiritual,' and at once expounded in practical and ethical terms.[48]

In simpler terms, Bruce writes that the "right knowledge" of God leads to "right behavior."[49] He further asserts, "For obedience to the knowledge of God which one has already received is a necessary and certain condition for the reception of further knowledge."[50] Christians, who do not use the knowledge they have gained through the Holy Spirit to live wise and spiritual lives, do not need additional knowledge. Like the fool of Old Testament Wisdom literature, they know the right thing to do but do not do it.

Evangelism depends on Christians living lives that are steeped in wisdom and abounding in good works. But the wisdom and works bear far greater fruits than we can imagine. Sure, we grow spiritually as a result of godly wisdom and works, but so does the church. The power of the gospel becomes palpable to those outside the church. When they see Christians living with joy, contentment, peace, and power that is foreign to their world, they are going to want it. But they will only see those things if we have grown spiritually enough to be able to demonstrate them every day, in every situation, and in every word.

---

[48] Ibid.
[49] Bruce, *Commentary on the Epistle to the Colossians*, 186.
[50] Ibid.

APPENDIX TWO

The Need for a New Educational Paradigm

The second consideration in developing a curriculum for spiritual disciplines is the need for a biblically-sound educational model. Due to the unique nature of Christian education in general and the very specific goal of spiritual disciplines, an educational philosophy must be followed that is thoroughly God-centered. George Knight challenges Christian educators to "individually examine their own basic beliefs in terms of reality, truth, and value, and then consciously build a personal philosophy upon that platform."[51] Knight further asserts that this philosophy will share much in common with theology since, from a Christian perspective, it must be grounded in the Bible that "sheds light on the issues of metaphysics, epistemology, and axiology."[52] However, as a model for understanding and teaching spiritual disciplines, it must also be highly practical so learning and spiritual growth can occur within "the everyday events of life."[53]

Writers teach readers how to practice spiritual disciplines using an educational model based on an unbiblical definition of spiritual disciplines. This incorrect definition causes teachers

---

[51] George R. Knight, *Philosophy & Education: An Introduction in Christian Perspective,* 4th ed. (Berrien Springs, MI: Andrews University Press, 2006), 166.

[52] Ibid., 168.

[53] Leslie Hardin, *Spirituality of Jesus: Nine Disciplines Christ Modeled for Us* (Grand Rapids: Kregel, 2009), 17.

to teach toward the wrong goals. If a teacher believes that spiritual disciplines are a means of grace, then he teaches his students to practice spiritual disciplines to gain grace. If this definition is wrong, then so is the goal. The methodology to arrive at that goal becomes ineffective if one changes the goal from "meriting grace" to becoming more Christlike in one's daily life. Therefore, an educational paradigm is needed that treats spiritual disciplines as uniquely spiritual, consistent with God's grand plan for Christianity, and that assists Christians in ordering and integrating their faith and their everyday lives.

Learning from Old Testament Wisdom Literature

As is often the case, the Bible provides its own best interpretation. Paul reminds Timothy, "All Scripture is inspired by God and profitable for teaching, for reproof, for correction, for training in righteousness" (2 Tim 3:16). Minimally, Paul would have had the Old Testament in mind when he made this statement, though it certainly extends to the New Testament as well. Paul believed that the Old Testament is essential to teach and mature Christians.

James Wilhoit recognizes the value of the Old Testament as a model for spiritual formation as well. He reframes Dallas Willard's "Curriculum for Christlikeness"[54] in four dimensions of spiritual formation: receiving, remembering, responding, and relating.[55] These four dimensions provide a potential pedagogical framework for Christian spiritual formation, which Wilhoit defines as (1) intentional; (2) communal; (3) requiring

---

[54] Dallas Willard, *The Divine Conspiracy: Rediscovering our Hidden Life in God* (San Francisco: Harper, 1997), 311-74.
[55] James Wilhoit, *Spiritual Formation As If the Church Mattered: Growing in Christ Through Community* (Grand Rapids: Baker, 2008), 50.

engagement; (4) accompanied by the Holy Spirit; (5) for the glory of God and the service of others; and (6) has as its means and end the imitation of Christ.[56] These six elements provide insights into a Christian praxis of spiritual formation using an educational model Wilhoit derived from Hebrew pedagogy.[57] Though insightful in his approach, Wilhoit focuses primarily on organizational goals and practices; therefore, the book is less useful for teaching the practices of the disciplines to individuals.

Klaus Issler also approaches spiritual formation with a philosophy consistent with the Old Testament. In particular, Issler's model views spiritual formation as increasing competencies in becoming like Jesus.[58] The idea of increasing competencies parallels the Hebrew understanding of *hochmah*, or wisdom. A wise man not only understands more about life, but he puts that understanding into practice—with growing expertise.[59] Issler sees the bottom line as "the core of childhood formation is primarily rule keeping, but the core of adult formation is growing into the way of wisdom, with a heart formed like Jesus'."[60] The remainder of his book addresses how one can gain proficiency through wisdom by living the life of Jesus. He does not, however, spend time developing this basic premise.

For a thorough development of Issler's premise, though written before Issler's book, one must turn to the work of Daniel Estes. In *Hear, My Son: Teaching and Learning in Proverbs 1-9* Estes analyzes the educational philosophy of

---

[56] Ibid., 23.

[57] Ibid., 105.

[58] Klaus Issler, *Living into the Life of Jesus* (Downers Grove, IL: IVP Press, 2012), 27.

[59] C. Hassell Bullock, *An Introduction to the Old Testament Poetic Books*, rev. ed. (Chicago: Moody, 1988), 22.

[60] Issler, *Living into the Life of Jesus*, 23.

the Old Testament wisdom literature found in Proverbs 1-9.[61] By examining the philosophical underpinnings of wisdom and comparing them to those of spirituality and spiritual disciplines, one finds significant similarities. Starting from their shared philosophy, the practical model Estes proposes can be adapted easily to the teaching of spiritual disciplines.

Worldview

Worldview is often defined as "how one sees the world" or "a way of looking at the world."[62] Nancy Pearcy, referring to the works of Abraham Kuyper and Herman Dooyeweerd, provides a definitively biblical worldview as "an outlook on life that gives rise to a distinctively Christian form of culture—with the important qualification that it's not merely the relativistic belief of a particular culture but is based on the very Word of God, true for all times and places."[63] She further states that a biblical worldview is only effective when a Christian willingly submits her mind to "the Lord of the universe—a willingness to be taught by Him."[64] Estes expresses this same commitment and outlines these elements in his study, as will be noted below.

As pointed out by Knight, the philosophical underpinnings of a worldview and its resultant educational philosophy consist of three parts, metaphysics, epistemology, and axiology. Metaphysics is the study of the nature of reality; epistemology, the study of the nature of truth and knowledge;

---

[61] Daniel Estes, *Hear, My Son: Teaching and Learning in Proverbs 1-9* (Downers Grove, IL: InterVarsity Press, 1997).

[62] Pearcy, *Total Truth*, 23.

[63] Ibid., 24.

[64] Ibid.

and axiology, the study of value.[65] In Estes' analysis, one finds all three of these categories present in his educational paradigm.

Estes begins by intentionally discussing the worldview found in Proverbs 1 – 9. The origin of the universe and all reality (metaphysics) is God.[66] That God is creator and sustainer is foundational to the wisdom writers' understanding of how the universe—and life itself—operates. Since God is Creator, he sovereignly controls every aspect of life, again showing the importance of metaphysics.[67] Even as God is in control, he chooses to reveal himself and his world in knowable, understandable ways—while at the same time maintaining a level of mysterious that is beyond human comprehension.[68] This understanding of God's revelation is the foundation of epistemology within wisdom literature. And finally, Estes asserts that humans, recognizing God's power and sovereignty, must reverence God.[69] As a normative statement, this conclusion serves as the axiological foundation for how believers should live.

In considering the use of this worldview for understanding and teaching spiritual disciplines, beginning at the end is helpful. Spiritual disciplines are acts of submission to and reverence for God. These acts are valuable because they assist the Christian in aligning their life and will with the sovereign creator of the universe. As Estes points out, "Because every facet of life has a religious dimension, wisdom calls its hearers to a whole-life response to Yahweh. In this worldview every action and choice in life, including even the most apparently

---

[65] Knight, *Philosophy & Education*, 9.
[66] Estes, *Hear, My Son*, 22-25.
[67] Ibid., 26-30.
[68] Ibid., 30-35.
[69] Ibid., 35-38.

mundane, is imbued with theological significance."[70] Estes' conclusion that wisdom calls believers to a "whole-life response" parallels the view presented within this book of spiritual disciplines as being "every action and choice in life."

Educational Values

By accepting the parallel, the metaphysical and epistemological assumptions may now be understood as valuable and relevant foundations for spiritual disciplines, and to do so is not difficult. Both wisdom and spirituality assume that God's way is always best. The foundation for that assumption is God as creator and God as sovereign. Both wisdom and spirituality assume that God's will and ways are knowable; otherwise there would be no purpose in pursuing them. However, as Estes posits, God's ways are only knowable through deep searching of his teachings, exercise of the truths gained, and toil and hard work.[71] One finds the same need for diligence, exercise, and hard work in many of the discussions of spirituality, spiritual disciplines, and godliness found in Paul's epistles.[72]

Based on the worldview described in Proverbs 1 – 9, Estes develops three specific ethical elements that guide the student of God's word and ways:

1. Humble willingness to accept instruction (paralleling *didache,* or "teachings").
2. Commitment to righteousness (paralleling *eusebeia,* or "godliness").

---

[70] Ibid., 36.

[71] Ibid., 31.

[72] For an excellent discussion on Paul's use of toil, labor, diligence, etc., see Victor Pfitzner, *Paul and the Agon Motif* (Boston: Brill Academic, 1997).

3. Life ordered by God's boundaries (paralleling *gymnasia*, or "exercise" or "discipline").[73]

Any student of wisdom or of spirituality and spiritual disciplines must ascribe to these three values. One can find all three of these values present in Paul's writings, particularly in the Pastorals. Paul exhorts Timothy to accept the instruction (*didache*) of the Lord and to pass it on to others who desire to learn (2 Tim 2:2). Further, Paul's call to godliness (*eusebeia*) in the Pastorals parallels wisdom's call to righteousness. And wisdom's admonition to live an orderly life in accordance with God's will parallels Paul's exhortation to discipline (*gymnasia*) oneself (1 Tim 4:7-8) and one's body (1 Cor 9:27).

Educational Goals

Estes continues in his analysis of educational paradigms by outlining the goals for education which he derives from wisdom literature. He identifies six goals from Proverbs that can serve as the goals for teaching the spiritual disciplines. These six goals are:

1. Commitment to a way of life.
2. Development of inner character.
3. Competence in understanding and living life.
4. Protection from the results of bad choices.
5. Prosperity (defined as shalom, or completeness and wholeness).
6. Knowledge of God as both transcendent and immanent.[74]

---

[73] Estes, *Hear, My Son*, 62.
[74] Ibid., 63-86.

When using a definition of spiritual discipline that seeks to integrate the spiritual disciplines into a daily walk with God, the goals for teaching them need to include changes in knowledge, attitude, behaviors, and life goals. Estes' list from Proverbs enumerates such goals. But again, these shared educational goals should not be a surprise given the worldview and values shared between wisdom and spirituality.

Roles of Teacher and Learner

While obvious differences in curriculum and instructional processes are evident, the roles of the teacher and of the learner are, again, very similar. Estes describes the teacher in Proverbs as a guide.[75] "The teacher is at times an expert, at times a facilitator, but always the guide, pointing the learners toward their own independent competence."[76] Ultimately, the teacher's goal is to have the learner reach maturity.

The learner is a disciple of God. Beyond simply learning about God or about God's creation, or even imitating the life of the teacher, the learner is called to interact with and acquire wisdom. Specifically, Estes describes four roles of the learner that find an almost perfect parallel to Paul's call to godliness in 1 Timothy 4:6-16. Specifically, what the learner is to do is:

Proverbs 1—9	1 Timothy 4:6-16
Receive Wisdom	Receive Godliness
Respond to Wisdom	Respond to/in Godliness
Value Wisdom	Value Godliness
Assimilate Wisdom[77]	Assimilate Godliness

---

[75] Ibid., 134.
[76] Ibid.
[77] Ibid., 135-149.

When considering how to live a life filled with godliness, which is the goal of spiritual discipline in 1 Timothy, Paul appears to draw from wisdom's paradigm: receive the instructions on godliness, respond to and in godliness through discipline, understand the value (profit) of godliness, and then "be absorbed in them so that your progress may be evident to all" (1 Tim 4:15). The process of becoming godly through the exercise of spiritual discipline is much the same as the process of becoming wise.

Heart-Deep Curriculum

Estes' paradigm provides a solid biblical foundation for approaching the teaching of spiritual disciplines. Using Proverbs, he answers the philosophical questions often neglected in the development of any curriculum, but especially curriculum concerning spiritual disciplines. However, while Estes' work is extremely biblical, theological, and philosophical, it lacks in the area of practicality. Estes does provide a few suggestions for the approach to the curriculum, process of instruction, and educational goals, but they are limited to their specific application in Proverbs. Estes himself concludes his book by asking questions about the legitimacy and appropriateness of using the model derived from Proverbs 1 – 9, intended for a Jewish nation in ancient Israel, in contemporary pedagogy.[78]

Since Estes' premise is that the goal of wisdom literature is to produce a "whole life response"[79] then a pedagogy that supports such a response would appear to be the most appropriate. In today's educational atmosphere of pragmatism and progressivism on one side and essentialism on the other, a

---

[78] Estes, *Hear, My Son,* 153.
[79] Ibid., 30.

model needs to be used that captures the heart of the learner and carries her on a journey deep into God's word and applies the discoveries along the way to every aspect of her life. Gary Newton presents such a model.

Newton states that the purpose of a comprehensive, heart-deep curriculum is to help "students design specific goals and objectives to live out their commitments in their everyday lives."[80] While Newton identifies the purpose with the final steps of a curriculum, that goal must also be present throughout the development of each lesson. What makes Newton's work particularly relevant to the study of spiritual disciplines is his model uses four domains of learning, cognitive, affective, volitional, and behavioral.[81]

The majority of Bible teaching takes place in the first domain, cognition. Well-meaning teachers emphasize the importance of the Bible through Scripture memorization, Bible drills, and Bible stories. Newton states that even the cognitive level is more than just rote memorization. Citing the work of Benjamin Bloom, Newton lists six levels of learning, knowledge, comprehension, application, analysis, synthesis, and evaluation.[82] What makes Newton's approach so relevant is that he adds a final level, "wisdom," which he defines as "the highest level of thinking related to putting knowledge into practice in making decisions."[83] Newton makes the same connection between learning and wisdom and a whole life change that Estes advocates from Proverbs 1 – 9.

---

[80] Gary Newton, *Heart-Deep Teaching: Engaging Students for Transformed Lives* (Nashville: Broadman and Holman, 2012), 195.
[81] Ibid., 45-54.
[82] Benjamin Bloom, *Taxonomy of Educational Objectives: The Classification of Educational Goals*, 1st ed. (New York: David McKay, 1956), 18, 90-93, quoted in Newton, 46.
[83] James Lee, *The Content of Religious Instruction* (Birmingham, AL: Religious Education Press, 1985), 159, quoted in Newton, 46.

The affective domain relates to the change in attitudes and emotions.[84] As a student learns from the Bible he becomes aware of how it might impact his Christian life. Though simple, this awareness can lead the Christian to pay more attention to what he is learning and how it can be applied in his life. Ultimately, he begins to assess situations and respond to them based on his growing understanding of God's word. Ultimately, as a student grows in the affective domain, a new worldview is formed.[85] This formation of a new worldview concurs with the goal in both wisdom and teachings on godliness to assimilate the teachings into a new way of viewing and evaluating life.

Changes in the volitional domain bring the individual's will into alignment with God's will.[86] For Estes, one of the values within wisdom literature is to bring one's life under the control of and live within the boundaries of the Creator.[87] The Apostle Paul's discussion of "disciplining oneself unto godliness" in 1 Timothy 4:7-8 has similar overtones where one must bring one's life under the authority of God for the benefit of salvation in this life and beyond.

Changes in the behavioral domain relate to the skills and competencies needed to accomplish the desired changes in one's life, especially as they relate to the other domains.[88] As learners advance through stages of behavioral growth, they become more adept at applying their knowledge and skills to their life circumstances. As the four domains begin to merge together in heart-deep learning, these skills find other applications in related life circumstances.[89] In

---

[84] Newton, *Heart-Deep Teaching*, 50.

[85] Ibid.

[86] Ibid., 52.

[87] Estes, *Hear, My Son*, 62.

[88] Newton, *Heart-Deep Teaching*, 52.

[89] Ibid., 53.

other words, heart-deep learning facilitates a "whole life response" to the word of God, whether those words are in the form of wisdom literature or teachings on spirituality and spiritual disciplines.

ADDITIONAL RESOURCES

Attridge, Harold W. *The Epistle to the Hebrews: A Commentary on the Epistle to the Hebrews*. Hermeneia. Philadelphia: Fortress Press, 1989.

Blackaby, Henry T. *Fresh Encounter: Experiencing God in Revival and Spiritual Awakening*. Nashville: Broadman & Holman, 1996.

Bloom, Benjamin. *Taxonomy of Educational Objectives: The Classification of Educational Goals*, 1st ed. New York: David McKay, 1956.

Boyer, Ernest. *A Way in the World: Family Life as Spiritual Discipline*. San Francisco: Harper & Row, 1984.

Bruce, F. F. *The Epistles to the Colossians, to Philemon, and to the Ephesians*. The New International Commentary on the New Testament. 1st Ed. Grand Rapids: Eerdmans, 1984.

_____.*The Epistle to the Hebrews*. The New International Commentary on the New Testament. Rev. ed. Grand Rapids: Eerdmans, 1990.

Bullock, C. Hassell. *An Introduction to the Old Testament Poetic Books*, Rev. ed. Chicago: Moody, 1988.

Calhoun, Adele Ahlberg. *Spiritual Disciplines Handbook: Practices that Transform Us.* Downers Grove, IL: InterVarsity Press, 2005.

Calvin, John. *On a Christian Life.* Grand Rapids: Christian Classics Ethereal Library. http://www.ccel.org/ccel/calvin/chr_life.pdf (accessed January 16, 2013).

Carson, D. A. *A Call to Spiritual Reformation: Priorities from Paul and His Prayers.* Grand Rapids: Baker Book House, 1992.

————. *Matthew.* In vol. 8 of *The Expositor's Bible Commentary.* Edited by Frank E. Gaebelein, 1-599. Grand Rapids: Zondervan, 1995.

————. "Spiritual Disciplines," *Themelios* 36, no. 3 (2011). http://thegospel coalition.org/themelios/article/spiritual_disciplines (accessed June 18, 2012).

————. "When is Spirituality Spiritual? Reflections of Some Problems of Definition," JETS 37, no. 3 (1994), 381-94.

Estep, James R., and Jonathan H. Kim, eds. *Christian Formation: Integrating Theology and Human Development.* Nashville: B&H Academic, 2010.

Estes, Daniel. *Hear, my Son: Teaching and learning in Proverbs 1—9.* Downers Grove, IL: Inter Varsity Press, 1997.

Fitzmyer, Joseph. *Romans.* The Anchor Bible. New York: Doubleday, 1993.

Foster, Richard J. *Celebration of Discipline: The Path to Spiritual Growth*. Rev. ed. San Francisco: Harper & Row, 1998.

France, R. T. *The Gospel of Matthew*. The New International Commentary on the New Testament. Rev. ed. Grand Rapids: Eerdmans, 2007.

Goheen, Keith. "Grieving as a Spiritual Discipline." *Chaplaincy Today* 25, no. 1 (2009), http://www.professionalchaplains. org/files/publications/ chaplaincy_today_online/ volume_25/number_1/25_1essaygoheen.pdf (accessed January 11, 2011).

Guthrie, George. *Hebrews*. The NIV Application Commentary. Grand Rapids: Zondervan, 1998.

Hagner, Donald Alfred. *Matthew 1-13*. Word Biblical Commentary. Dallas: Word Books, 1993.

_____. *Matthew 14-28*. Word Biblical Commentary. Dallas: Word Books, 1995.

Hardin, Leslie T. *The Spirituality of Jesus: Nine Disciplines Christ Modeled for Us*. Grand Rapids: Kregel, 2009.

Haykin, Michael A. G. *The God Who Draws Near: An Introduction to Biblical Spirituality*. Webster, NY: Evangelical Press, 2007.

Henderson, Daniel. *Fresh Encounters: Experiencing Transformation Through United Worship-Based Prayer*. Colorado Springs: NavPress, 2008.

Hickman, Richard Francis. "Experiencing the Absolute: the Ecumenical Basis of Spiritual Discipline." *Dialogue & Alliance* 3, no. 4 (1990): 4–13.

Issler, Klaus. *Living into the Life of Jesus.* Downers Grove, IL: IVP Press, 2012.

Knight, George W. *The Pastoral Epistles.* The New International Greek Testament Commentary. Grand Rapids: Eerdmans, 1992.

Lausanne Movement, The. "Lausanne Covenant." http://www.lausanne.org/en/ documents/lausanne-covenant.html (accessed August 11, 2012).

Lee, James. *The Content of Religious Instruction.* Birmingham, AL: Religious Education Press, 1958.

Luz, Ulrich. *Matthew 21-28.* Hermeneia. Philadelphia: Fortress Press, 2005.

Malphurs, Aubrey. *Advanced Strategic Planning: A Model for Church and Ministry Leaders.* Grand Rapids: Baker Books, 2005.

Marasco, Ron, and Carolyn D. Roark. "Acting as Spiritual Discipline: An Interview with Ron Marasco." *Ecumenica* 1, no. 1 (2008): 61–72.

Merritt, Barbara W. "Ministry as Spiritual Discipline." *Unitarian Universalist Christian* 43, no. 1 (1988): 14–20.

Moo, Douglas J. *The Letters to the Colossians and to Philemon*. Pillar New Testament. Grand Rapids: Eerdmans, 2008.

_____.*The Epistle to the Romans*. New International Commentary on the New Testament. Rev. ed. Grand Rapids: Eerdmans, 1996.

Mounce, Robert. *Romans*. The New American Commentary. Nashville: Broadman & Holman, 1995.

Mounce, William D. *Pastoral Epistles*. Word Biblical Commentary. Nashville: Nelson, 2000.

Murray, John. *The Epistle to the Romans*. New International Commentary on the New Testament. Rev. ed. Grand Rapids: Eerdmans, 1968.

Nassif, Bradley, ed. *Four Views on Christian Spirituality*. Grand Rapids: Zondervan, 2012.

Newton, Gary. *Heart Deep Teaching: Engaging Students for Transformed Lives*. Nashville: Broadman and Holman, 2012.

Nouwen, Henri J. M. "Spiritual Direction." *Worship* 55, no. 5 (1981): 399–404.

Pazmino, Robert. *God Our Teacher: Theological Basics in Christian Education*. Grand Rapids: Baker, 2001.

Pearcy, Nancy. *Total Truth: Liberating Christianity From Its Cultural Captivity*. Wheaton, IL: Crossway, 2005.

Pfizner, Victor. *Paul and the Agon Motif.* Boston: Brill Academic, 1997.

Powell, Kara, and Dick Chapa. *Sticky Faith.* Grand Rapids: Zondervan, 2011.

Schreiner, Thomas. *Romans,* Baker Exegetical Commentary on the New Testament. Grand Rapids: Baker, 1998.

Schweer, G. William. "Evangelism." In *Holman Bible Dictionary.* Edited by Trent Butler. Nashville: Broadman and Holman, 1991.

Stott, John. *The Message of Romans.* Downers Grove, IL: InterVarsity Press, 1994.

Towner, Philip H. *The Letters to Timothy and Titus.* New International Commentary on the New Testament. Rev. ed. Grand Rapids: Eerdmans, 2006.

United States Catholic Conference, Inc. *Catechism of the Catholic Church,* 2nd ed. New York: Doubleday, 1994.

Waterworth, J. ed and trans. *The Council of Trent: The Cannons and Decrees of the Sacred and Oecumenical Council of Trent.* London: Dolman, 1848. http://history.hanover.edu/texts/trent/trentall.html (accessed October 21, 2013).

Whitney, Donald S. *Spiritual Disciplines for the Christian Life.* Colorado Springs: NavPress, 1997.

_____. *Spiritual Disciplines Within the Church: Participating Fully in the Body of Christ.* Chicago: Moody Press, 1996.

_____. "Teaching Spiritual Disciplines," Class lecture, DMin 80913: Biblical Spirituality in the Local Church, The Southern Baptist Theological Seminary, Louisville, KY, January 11, 2013).

Wilhoit, James. *Spiritual Formation As If the Church Mattered: Growing in Christ Through Community.* Grand Rapids: Baker, 2008.

Willard, Dallas. *The Divine Conspiracy: Rediscovering Our Hidden Life in God.* San Francisco: Harper, 1998.

_____. *The Spirit of the Disciplines: Understanding How God Changes Lives.* San Francisco: Harper & Row, 1988.

Wright, N. T. *Colossians and Philemon.* Tyndale New Testament Commentaries. Downers Grove, IL: IVP Academic, 2008.